LIFE&

DEATH

THE POWER OF WORDS

Rob McCorkle

BECOMING LOVE MEDIA GROUP

www.BecomingLoveMinistries.com

BECOMING LOVE MEDIA GROUP

CONTENTS

ACKNOWLEDGEMENTS

I'm grateful for Becoming Love Ministries Association
who blesses me with time to write.

I'm grateful for the encouraging words
of Craig Rench who has inspired me to write.

I'm grateful for my wife who supports me,
making it easier to write.

Finally, I'm grateful to the work of the
Holy Spirit who sources me
so I'm enabled to write.

INTRODUCTION

Writing about transforming our words has not been undertaken because I've mastered the use of my tongue, quite the contrary. Transforming my words has been a marathon. My undergraduate work in college, a Bachler of Arts degree in Communications, unveiled the power of speech. We plumbed the influence of communicators and examined how words both heal and hurt.

Following college, I married, started a family, and entered full-time ministry. I wish I could say that my knowledge of the power of words was perfectly demonstrated on every occasion. But I failed more times than I care to admit in speaking the right words in all three arenas of my life: marriage, family, and the church.

Of course, there were moments when I communicated well—waxed eloquently, as we used to say in our seminary preaching class. But daily life revealed that I could digress into complaining or negative speech at the sight of traffic jams or long lines at a grocery store. Beware if I became frustrated with a staff member at church or a neighbor down the street because I could become an oozie of poisonous words.

The Bible has much to say about our speech. One of the most significant Scriptures says, "Death and life are in the power of the tongue, and those who love it will eat its fruit" (Proverbs

18:21). The Good News Translation says, "What you say can preserve life or destroy it; so you must accept the consequences of your words." There is no such thing as a neutral word. Every word released from your mouth can and will preserve life or destroy it.

Over the years, I've watched marriages crash, children become withdrawn, and churches fragment and split—all from inappropriate and destructive words released from the mouths of people. The same results occur from the lack of appropriate words being spoken at the right moment. If you withhold encouraging, life-giving words from someone long enough, it can suffocate their emotional health. I'll say it again: there is no such thing as a neutral word. Therefore, we need supernatural help to consistently speak words that encourage, edify, and exhort people as well as honor the Lord. How can we do this?

First, transformation must begin in our hearts. Jesus said, "For the mouth speaks out of that which fills the heart" (Matthew 12:34b). Our hearts leak through our mouths. Therefore, all sin, anger, bitterness, and unforgiveness—anything unlike Christ—must be cleansed from our hearts through the power of the Holy Spirit (see Ephesians 4:32). A heart that is clean and filled with the presence of the Spirit is sourced to release words filled with life.

Second, we must remain totally dependent upon the guidance and leadership of the Holy Spirit if we ever hope to speak timely and beneficial words. Jesus said, "But the Helper, the Holy Spirit, whom the Father will send in My name, He will teach you all things" (John 14:26a).

Discipline and restraint may work for a season, but ultimately, we need the supernatural power of the Spirit sourcing us if we desire to effectively communicate. Note what Jesus said: "[the Spirit] will teach you *all* things." That includes using words: He will teach you when to speak, where to speak, and what to speak. Even Jesus didn't speak on His own initiative; He was sourced by the Father for His words to be filled with life (see John 6:63 and 12:49). Therefore, we must have the Helper—the Holy Spirit—guiding our words.

Third, we need training. We train for many things in life, and we'll pay large sums of money to be adequately equipped mentally, financially, and physically. On almost every street corner, there is a health club promising a stronger, healthier body in a matter of months. What about training our tongues?

Would you enroll in a course that could train you to use life-giving words or tether you to Scripture concerning the use of your mouth? Is there a daily study-guide that could help you eliminate destructive words from your life and foster words that reflect the heart and nature of God? Those questions prompted the study that you are beginning entitled, *Life and Death: The Power of Words*.

The book and study-guide can be used in two ways: first, you can use it as a twenty-one-day spiritual journey in which you daily complete one chapter and answer the questions at the end of the lesson. Second, you can choose a twenty-one-week spiritual journey. If you choose this option, then you would read one chapter and complete the questions over the course of one week. The advantage with this option is that it facilitates an in-depth examination on various aspects of your use of words.

Either choice requires a commitment and an investment of not only time but obedience. All of us will stand before the Lord and give an account, Jesus said, of "every careless word" that is spoken (Matthew 12:36). A careless (*argos*) word refers to a word that is useless or barren. It's like planting a seed that doesn't have the capacity to germinate and produce a harvest. Speaking lifeless words is a serious offense for a follower of Christ. Consider this journey as "tongue training" to help you learn to speak words that will produce a harvest of righteousness. In time, you, and those around you, will see the difference.

Most of all, your words will reflect the character of Jesus whose every word was spirit and life (see John 6:63).

LESSON 1

Killing the Flesh

Throughout the New Testament Gospels, contrasts are often used for teaching purposes. For example, the two sisters in Luke 10:39–40 help us to understand the difference between a listening and a distracted heart. Or the parable of the two sons in Luke 15:11–32 contrasts the attitudes of two sons and the value of something that was lost but later found. In Luke 18:9–17, we read the story of two worshippers that underscores the value of true humility before the Lord.

These and many other examples paint a picture of the contrast between two opposing factors, which enables us to make a proper choice. In many cases, we learn the right or wrong way to think, act, and live and the potential consequences of each.

Concerning the use of our tongues, we can be influenced either by the Spirit or the flesh. Jesus said, "It is the Spirit who gives life; the flesh profits nothing; the words that I have spoken to you are spirit and are life" (John 6:63). This verse frames a contrast between the flesh and the Spirit. Only the Spirit, Jesus said, can impart life. The Spirit rejuvenates, activates, and energizes both people and elements. In Genesis 1:2, we see the

Spirit described as moving over the surface of the waters. This means to wait with anticipation. Some scholars liken the word moving to an anxious eagle expecting her eggs to soon hatch.

What was the Spirit of God anxiously waiting for? The answer is found in Genesis 1:3, the release of the Word of God. The moment God released a word, the Spirit activated that word, and creation occurred. From light to sea creatures, vegetation to human beings, the Spirit of God activated every spoken word of God. Perhaps Jesus had creation in mind when He said in John 6:63, "It is the Spirit who gives life," because the Spirit was the power source who energized the Word.

Perhaps Jesus thought about Ezekiel who commanded the Spirit to enter a pile of brittle bones transforming a dry heap into a living army (see Ezekiel 37:9–10). Once again, the Spirit imparted life. The Bible is filled with examples of the Spirit giving life to dead bodies, twisted limbs, mute tongues, and sin-filled hearts. The flesh profits nothing because only the Spirit gives life.

When using the word flesh (*sarx*), Jesus had in mind the sinful human nature which is void of God. The flesh is carnal, self-centered, arrogant, and very destructive. Left to the devices of the flesh, we will fail to honor God or value people. Sinful flesh is only concerned with self-preservation. Flesh prompted words, therefore, can be cruel and vindictive. We've heard the saying, "Sticks and stones may break my bones, but words will never hurt me." That little phrase is false. It's better stated, "Sticks and stones may bruise my skin, but words will hurt me deep within."

Words prompted by the flesh have caused great harm to people, organizations, and communities. The Proverb writer stated that death and life are in the power of the tongue (Proverbs 18:21). Remember in the Introduction, we emphasized that words are never neutral. Words either give or take life; there's no middle ground. If then, our words are motivated by the sinful flesh, be assured they will be very destructive wherever they land.

Just in the book of Proverbs alone, we see that words can conceal violence (10:11), bring ruination (10:14), destroy neighbors (11:9), stir up anger (15:1), spout folly (15:2), crush the spirit (15:4), bring strife (18:6), and snare the soul (18:7). In contrast, words can be a fountain of life (10:11), contain discernment (10:13), be choice silver (10:20), feed many (10:21), flow with wisdom (10:31), and bring forth what is acceptable (10:32). What determines the difference in our words? According to Jesus the difference rests in what sources them.

The words Jesus spoke were never sourced by the flesh, but they were sourced by the Spirit and, therefore, produced life with profound results. When Jesus spoke, nature was affected, twisted limbs were made straight, disease left bodies, demons fled, and dead things lived again. His words contained power because they were sourced by the Holy Spirit. In fact, Jesus never spoke on His own initiative but only when heaven prompted Him (see John 12:49). Just imagine what your life might look like if you never spoke until the Spirit gave you something to say.

I was raised in a church that emphasized a life of holiness. That term can raise many different images in people's minds, but the most accurate picture of what it means to live a holy life is found in Jesus. Holiness in its simplest definition is

Christlikeness. Every disciple is to look just like their teacher (see Luke 6:40); therefore, we should all look and act just like Him. Among other things, this includes the way we speak. If every word Jesus spoke was sourced by the Spirit, then the goal for our lives should be the same. We must learn to speak *only* as the Spirit prompts us. When we do, the results will be transforming.

Speaking by the Spirit requires us to do something about the flesh, however. There's an old saying, "What you tolerate will dominate." The sinful flesh is not something you can live with because it will always rise and control your life and words.

The Bible is very clear concerning the flesh, "Now those who belong to Christ Jesus have crucified the flesh with its passions and desires" (Galatians 5:24). Although this verse indicates a moment of choice to end the tyranny of flesh, it does not eliminate the need to grow, learn, and mature in our Christian walk. In fact, in this same passage the writer goes on to instruct, "If we live by the Spirit, let us also walk by the Spirit" (Galatians 5:25). The word walk means to follow, abide, or remain in agreement with something. The truth is, if we ever hope to consistently speak under the influence of the Spirit, then we must die to our flesh and continue following the Holy Spirit every moment of our lives.

May today be the dawn of Spirit-sourced words in your life. Make the decision to crucify the flesh and begin walking in total agreement with the Holy Spirit. May every word you speak be filled with the Spirit and with life.

QUESTIONS

1. What is the Holy Spirit saying to you about the words proceeding from your mouth? Are they being sourced by the Spirit or flesh?

2. How different would your life and relationships be if you crucified your flesh?

3. What would your day look like if you only spoke as the Spirit inspired you?

> If you choose to extend this lesson for one week, then complete the following questions and applications each day.

DAY 2

QUESTIONS
& Applications

1. Reflecting on yesterday, in what ways were you like Jesus in the words you spoke? Did you speak in the flesh or Spirit? Describe your experience.

2. Read Galatians 5:16–25.

3. Reflecting on Galatians 5:19–21, in what ways are the deeds of the flesh evident through words that you speak?

4. Prayer for today: *Lord, may I walk in the Spirit today.*

DAY 3 QUESTIONS
& Applications

1. Reflecting on Galatians 5:22–23, in what way is the fruit of the Spirit evident through words?

2. Based on the words you used recently, was the fruit of the Spirit evident? Describe your experience.

3. Prayer for today: *Lord, may my words today demonstrate the fruit of the Spirit.*

DAY 4 QUESTIONS
& Applications

1. Reflecting on Galatians 5:17, have you ever experienced a battle between the flesh and the Spirit? If so, discuss the battle and results.

2. Reflecting on Galatians 5:24, what do you think it means to crucify the flesh?

3. Reflecting on Galatians 5:25, describe how you can consistently walk in the Spirit? What does walking in the Spirit and speaking in the Spirit have in common?

4. Prayer for today: *Lord, source my words as I walk in the Spirit.*

DAY 5 — QUESTIONS & Applications

1. In Galatians 5:20, an outburst of anger is identified as a deed of the flesh. Is it possible to be angry and not sin with our words? Describe your experiences.

2. Was Jesus ever angry? If so, how did He use His words in that moment?

3. How did Jesus handle difficult situations? Does your life resemble His (see Luke 6:40)?

4. Prayer for today: *Lord, enable me to be just like you.*

DAY 6 — QUESTIONS & Applications

1. Jesus spoke words of life; therefore, amazing things happened when He spoke. Describe some amazing things that have occurred through your words.

2. Jesus only spoke as the Father spoke to Him (see John 12:49). Has that happened in your life? How can you learn to hear the Father speak more clearly to you?

3. Prayer for today: *Lord, help me to hear you better today.*

DAY 7 — QUESTIONS
& Applications

1. Reflecting on this last week, in what ways have you spoken in the Spirit?

2. Describe what has been the greatest lesson you have learned this week.

3. Prayer for today: *Lord, may your Holy Spirit be the source of all my words.*

LESSON 2

The Heart of the Issue

Have you ever spent much time gardening? Growing up, I had the blessing of eating food from my grandfather's garden, and when we bought our first house, I tilled the ground and became a green thumb. In all honesty, gardening was more difficult than I thought. There was much to learn about the condition of soil, controlling garden pests, preventing plant diseases, various watering techniques, and when and how to harvest a crop. There was one thing, however, that was always certain: what I sowed is what I reaped.

Not one time in eighteen years of gardening did I sow beans and harvest cucumbers. I never planted corn and reaped beans. My fruit always gave evidence to the nature of the seed. In addition, what I harvested indicated the health of the plant. In other words, fruit doesn't lie. Healthy fruit is produced by a healthy root.

Jesus essentially said the same thing about our words. Our words tell the truth about what we are rooted in revealing the nature of our hearts. If you shake a cup of water, you can expect water to spill out. What spills from the cup is not determined by the shaking; rather, it's determined by the contents. The shaking merely reveals the nature of what's inside the cup. Milk, tea, soda pop—it doesn't matter—what spills is only determined by what is inside. Likewise, our mouths reveals the contents of our hearts. The words that spill from our mouths are not determined by the agitation but by what we are full of.

Both in the church and in society, people blame others for the words they use. Someone blaming a verbal tirade on the actions of another is failing to take responsibility for what is inside the heart. The truth is, other people are often used to reveal the true nature of our hearts. Henry Cloud said, "Our words do not come from somewhere outside us, as if we were a ventriloquist's dummy. They are the product of our heart."[1] You might think your spouse, children, or employer causes you to speak careless words, but maybe it's really revealing to you something about the contents of your cup.

Some of the clearest teaching about words proceeding from our hearts came from Jesus. He said,

> Either make the tree good and its fruit good, or make the tree bad and its fruit bad; for the tree is known by its fruit. You brood of vipers, how can you, being evil, speak what is good? For the mouth speaks out of that which fills the heart. The good man brings out of *his* good treasure what is good; and the evil man brings out of *his* evil treasure what is evil. But I tell you that every careless word that people speak, they shall give an accounting for it in the day of

judgment. For by your words, you will be justified, and by your words you will be condemned
(Matthew 12:33–37).

When Jesus said a tree is known by its fruit, He was explain-
ing how the contents of our hearts are revealed. In this context,
He was addressing a group of religious leaders who were inca-
pable of speaking healthy words because their hearts were evil.
Therefore, everything they said was poisoned. Regardless of
their religious status or their outward appearance, their words
revealed the actual condition of their hearts.

Jesus used the word treasure (*thesauros*) when He spoke of
things in our hearts. Most people recognize that word because
a thesaurus is a book of synonyms, a treasury of words. The
Greek word is defined as a depository where a person stores
priceless treasures. In Matthew 2:11, the Magi worshipped
Jesus and then opened their treasures (*thesauros*) to give Him
gifts of gold, frankincense, and myrrh. These priceless items
were kept in a depository.

However, the same Greek word *thesauros* can be defined as
a casket. This suggests a box containing something that is dead
and decayed. A good man, then, will speak good things because
his depository is filled with priceless treasures, meaning his
heart is filled with righteousness. But an evil person is defined
as one who speaks from an evil depository, so this describes a
person whose heart is filled with unrighteousness. The question
is, what do your words reveal about your heart?

A depository filled with evil things will produce careless
(*argos*) words. A careless word is idle, inactive, barren, and life-

less. Careless words don't edify, encourage, inspire, or honor other people. Speaking careless words is like planting seeds that don't have the capacity to germinate and produce a healthy crop. The seed, no matter how carefully placed in the soil or tended, simply rots in the soil.

It's no different when we speak careless words to another person. We just might cause the soul of a person to become spiritually ill when they hear our barren words. We can be sure that we will not impart life to others if our words are careless. Worse still, it's an indicator that we're storing decayed things in our hearts.

Therefore, Jesus said we would be held accountable and be condemned for speaking careless words. Careless words not only affect other people in a negative manner, but they also point to the fact that our hearts need spiritual attention. Careless words cannot be blamed on other people; rather, a constant stream of them indicates that something is dead in our hearts. David cried out, "Create in me a clean heart, O God" (Psalm 51:10a). Perhaps it's time for you to let the Lord examine your heart, and should there be some old decaying things in your depository, then allow Him to give you a clean heart.

Our hope is, by the fruit of our words we will be known as sons and daughters of righteousness. And by our words, we will be justified because they testify to a heart that has been cleansed from all defilement and decay.

QUESTIONS

1. By your words, what are you known for? How would your family or coworkers describe the content of your words?

2. What kind of fruit do your words produce? Is it good or bad fruit? Explain.

3. What must change in your life so that each day you'll be justified by your words?

> If you choose to extend this lesson for one week, then complete the following questions and applications each day.

DAY 2 QUESTIONS
& Applications

1. When you are agitated by other people, what usually proceeds from your mouth?

2. Read Psalm 139:23–24. What are your observations about those verses?

3. Ask the Lord to search your heart. Are there some issues, attitudes, motives, or sins that He needs to cleanse?

4. Prayer for today: *Lord, give me a pure heart.*

DAY 3 QUESTIONS
& Applications

1. Reflecting on the day before, what did your words reveal about your heart? Explain your experiences.

2. Read Proverbs 4:23. What is the Holy Spirit saying to you about this verse?

3. What are some ways you can watch over your heart?

4. Prayer for today: *Lord, give me strength to guard my heart.*

DAY 4 QUESTIONS
& Applications

1. Read Matthew 12:33–37. What are your observations from these verses?

2. Why did Jesus call the Pharisees a brood of vipers? What do you think that means?

3. Prayer for today: *Lord, may my words give life and not take life.*

DAY 5   QUESTIONS
& Applications

1. Jesus said, "For the mouth speaks out of that which fills the heart" (Matthew 12:34b). What are some ways you can fill our hearts with the right things?

2. Can you identify three specific things that you will do today to fill your heart with what is good?

3. Reflecting on Matthew 12:37, what does it mean to be justified by your words?

4. Prayer for today: *Lord, fill my heart with your Holy Spirit.*

DAY 6   QUESTIONS
& Applications

1. Reflecting on Matthew 12:36, what are some examples of careless (idle) words?

2. How do you spiritually recover when careless words are spoken over you?

3. Are you learning to speak with life-giving words? Why or why not?

4. Prayer for today: *Lord, enable me to speak with words of life.*

DAY 7

QUESTIONS
& Applications

1. Reflecting on this last week, how did the Holy Spirit help you avoid speaking careless words? Did you fill your heart with good things? If so, how? If not, why?

2. What has been the greatest lesson you have learned this week?

3. How can you help others learn to speak with life giving words?

4. Prayer for today: *Lord, my heart belongs solely to you.*

LESSON 3

Unwholesome Words

Several years ago, someone described me as a "word nerd." I don't reject that title because it reveals a desire of my heart. I have a growing interest in the meaning of words, particularly those used in the Bible. Why are certain words used? How are they used? What is the context in which they're used, and what is the actual definition? These questions swirl around in my mind whenever I read Scripture. It is challenging for me to simply read through the Bible because I must investigate the words, their origin, their background, etc.

While reading the book of Ephesians, my interest became heightened as I came to 4:29 that says, "Let no unwholesome word proceed from your mouth, but only such *a word* as is good for edification according to the need *of the moment*, so that it will give grace to those who hear." Unwholesome? That word carries many different meanings. Unwholesome food bankrupts our health. Unwholesome water can pass along contaminates, parasites, and diseases. Ultimately, both unwholesome food and water can cause death.

From a standard dictionary we learn that the word unwholesome is an adjective and that it is defined as something detrimental to a person's physical, mental, or moral well-being. Synonyms of unwholesome are corrupt, loathsome, unsound, and noxious. Words used in other translations of the Bible for unwholesome are foul, dirty, harmful, evil, abusive, worthless, and corrupt. The Greek word for unwholesome is *sapros*. It's used eight times in the New Testament, one time by the apostle Paul in Ephesians 4:29 and seven times by Jesus referring to bad fruit, bad trees, and bad fish.

The meaning of *sapros* is rotten or putrid, and it stems from a root word that means septic. Given the historical setting of Ephesus, we have insight into why the apostle Paul may have chosen this word (unwholesome). The city of Ephesus was a wealthy metropolis. It contained one of the seven wonders of the world, a temple dedicated to a goddess named Artemis. In the shadow of this demonic temple, witchcraft and divination were rampant. The streets were filled with immoral, sex-driven prostitutes, and promiscuous activity openly occurred day and night.

The culture in and around Ephesus was, therefore, *septic*. Peppered throughout this massive city were dedicated Christ followers who had turned their backs on the prominent cultic practices and the moral depravity so common in those living in Ephesus. In Ephesians 4:25–32, Paul alerted believers to his concerns for those living in Ephesus. He addressed inauthenticity (verse 25), unresolved conflicts (verse 26), giving access to the enemy (verse 27), an unproductive lifestyle (verse 28), grieving the Spirit (verse 30), releasing wrong attitudes (verse 31), and the need for forgiveness (verse 32).

Amid this list, Paul challenged these Christians not to release unwholesome words from their mouths. It would have been easy for their words to become an echo of the culture. The environment was steeped with rotten, septic speech, but within the community of faith, believers were to speak differently. It's no different today. We are surrounded by immorality everywhere, and all too often the language and words used when speaking *to* people and *about* people are unwholesome. The larger concern, however, is how we speak and the words that proceed from our mouths.

If you consider the danger of raw sewage, you can then begin to understand the damage rotten, septic speech can have upon people. Jesus spoke strongly about causing a young believer to stumble (see Matthew 18:6). Very few things are more detrimental to young Christians than exposure to an unwholesome conversation spoken by other Christ followers. In future lessons we'll explore the harm that comes from gossip, slander, and deceptive words that sadly proceed from the mouth of believers. As Christ followers, whether in or out of the church walls, we must not allow unwholesome words to proceed from our mouths.

The question to consider is, have you become an echo of the culture or a voice that reflects your citizenship in heaven? Please don't blame your septic speech on the environment you live or work in, either. Christians are notorious for saying, "That's just the way they talk at the office," or "All the guys use that kind of language." As believers, we cannot allow the surrounding culture to influence the words that we use; our mouth must be governed by the Lord. David's cry for help should be just as relevant for us in this hour: "Set a guard, O Lord, over my mouth; keep watch over the door of my lips" (Psalm 141:3).

According to Ephesians 4:29, unwholesome words should be replaced with edifying words. Edifying words are filled with truth and have no hint of deception or flattery. I believe edifying words are released in love. They are not prompted by anger, frustration, or the need to impress; rather, we're compelled by love when speaking. Finally, I believe edifying words impart grace to those who hear. Grace enables people to become better than they are. Grace empowers people with hope, inspiration, and life.

Take inventory of the words you use. Examine conversations you've had with people at work, on the phone, with family members, in the lobby at church, or standing in a grocery line. Perhaps today becomes the day you submit your mouth to only speak edifying words instead of unwholesome ones.

May the Lord guard our mouths and watch over the doors of our lips.

QUESTIONS

1. Are your words unwholesome? And if so, why?

2. What's your action plan to speak only words of grace?

3. Is there anyone in your life whom you need to forgive?

If you choose to extend this lesson for one week, then complete
the following questions and applications each day.

DAY 2 — QUESTIONS
& Applications

1. Read Ephesians 4:25–32.

2. How do these verses influence our speech in a positive or negative way?

3. Prayer for today: *Lord, set a guard over my mouth.*

DAY 3 — QUESTIONS
& Applications

1. Reflecting on Ephesians 4:26, has unresolved conflict influenced your speech? If so, explain.

2. Reflecting on Ephesians 4:27, how does the enemy influence the words that you use?

3. Prayer for today: *Lord, let my speech be influenced by you.*

DAY 4 — QUESTIONS & Applications

1. Reflecting on Ephesians 4:29–30, do unwholesome words grieve the Holy Spirit? If so, how?

2. Reflecting on Ephesians 4:31, how can the attitudes identified influence your words?

3. Reflecting on Ephesians 4:32, how would this verse change the way you speak?

4. Prayer for today: *Lord, free my heart from all wrong attitudes.*

DAY 5 — QUESTIONS & Applications

1. What are some examples of unwholesome words you've heard? Do you speak unwholesome words?

2. What does it mean to speak edifying words?

3. Have you spoken edifying words in the last few days? Why or why not?

4. Prayer for today: *Lord, empower me to speak edifying words.*

DAY 6 — QUESTIONS & Applications

1. What is your response to unwholesome words from other believers?

2. How can you speak edifying words to someone without using flattery?

3. Has anyone ever spoken edifying words to you? If so, what was the result for you?

4. Prayer for today: *Lord, may my words become a source of grace.*

DAY 7 — QUESTIONS & Applications

1. Reflecting on this week, have your words been edifying to others? Why or why not?

2. What can you do to speak edifying words all the days of your life?

3. Read Psalm 141:3.

4. Prayer for today: *Lord, with your help I'll never speak an unwholesome word.*

LESSON 4

Two-Faced

Have you ever heard a person being described as two-faced? It's certainly not a compliment. The term describes someone who is "duplicitous." Duplicity is defined as something that is contradictory or a doubleness in thought, action, or speech. One definition describes duplicity this way: it is speaking out of two sides of your mouth. In terms of speech, if a person is duplicitous, then they will say one thing with one group of people and something entirely different when surrounded by another audience. Author Frank Viola wrote an interesting blog along these lines. Here's a portion:

> Several months ago, I was sitting in the lobby of a business waiting for an appointment. I could hear a conversation going on in another room between two women. They had no idea I could hear them, but the door was open, and they weren't whispering. From the sound of their voices and their vocabulary, I presume both women were in their mid-twenties. During the conversation, one of the women was talking about a friend of

hers. She was clearly distraught. The conversation went like this, "Yeah, she stabbed me in the back. I couldn't believe the things she was saying about me. And she's one of those Christians. They are so two-faced." The other woman responded, "I know what you mean! I've had the same experience. And they are the ones who think they are so righteous, judging everyone else for what they're doing wrong." The other woman replied, "I know, right?"[2]

The concept of being two-faced is found in the Bible. James 1:8 uses the term double-minded (*dipsuchos*). This compound word means two souls or two minds. The way they speak is inconsistent. James described a double-minded person as being unstable in all his ways. Throughout this epistle we discover examples of a believer's instability when they have a double mind. For example, they pray yet have no faith (1:6), they hear the word yet fail to obey (1:22), they declare love for God yet neglect the poor (2:3), and they declare their faith, yet it's not backed by works (2:14).

Nowhere is two-faced duplicity more evident than in the use of our mouths. James wrote, "With it we bless *our* Lord and Father, and with it we curse men, who have been made in the likeness of God; from the same mouth come *both* blessing and cursing. My brethren, these things ought not to be this way" (James 3:9–10). What James described in these verses is a two-faced believer who worships God on Sunday and speaks slanderous words about people on Monday.

One of the greatest criticisms concerning the lack of Christian integrity occurs when believers speak out of both sides of their mouths. For example, they talk about their relationships with God and still participate in gossip at work. Unchurched people hear that, and it registers as inconsistency in their minds. Even with little to no Christian training, a nonbeliever can recognize unstable, duplicitous actions in a Christ follower. Your mouth will always give you away.

In James 3:11–12, James identified four things in the natural world that cannot happen. First, a fountain cannot produce two types of water: fresh and bitter. Second, a fig tree will not produce olives. Third, a vine will not produce figs. Fourth, salt water will not produce fresh water. If those things cannot occur in the natural world, then they shouldn't happen in the spiritual world. No one who identifies himself as a Spirit-filled believer should use his mouth in a manner contrary to his redeemed nature.

Your life and witness should back up your mouth. We can't picture Jesus telling the religious leaders one thing and then saying something contradictory to His followers. In fact, Jesus asked His audience, "Which one of you convicts Me of sin? If I speak truth, why do you not believe Me" (John 8:46)? There was no sin found in Jesus. Every word He spoke was consistent with His lifestyle, and as a result He never spoke out of two sides of His mouth. Jesus is not just our example; He has filled us with Himself, thus enabling us to replicate Him.

If you say you are going to do something, then follow through with action. If you say you won't do something, then back it up by how you live. If you say you love God, then demonstrate it by how you love people. If you say you're a follower of Christ, then make sure your words are filled with life. You should be known as a person of integrity. Someone who is integrous lives a life of consistency in what they say and do. Stated differently, they are the same person privately as they say they are publicly.

James has a solution for an unstable, duplicitous believer. He said, "Draw near to God and He will draw near to you. Cleanse your hands, you sinners; and purify your hearts, you double-minded" (James 4:8). According to James, turning your double mind into a single mind requires three steps. First, get as close to God as you can. In fact, develop a lifestyle of intimacy with the Father just like Jesus did. Second, wash your hands of all known sin. Third, ask the Lord to purify your heart from all duplicity. Only the Lord can take a duplicitous believer who is unstable in all his ways and give him a single heart that is fully devoted to Him.

From this day forward, may you never be described as a two-faced believer. May the words you speak be demonstrated in your lifestyle.

QUESTIONS

1. Do your words indicate duplicity? If so, why?

2. Are people attracted to Christ or repelled by the things you say? How can you tell the difference?

3. What are some characteristics of a single-minded believer?

If you choose to extend this lesson for one week, then complete the following questions and applications each day.

DAY 2 QUESTIONS
& Applications

1. How would you describe someone who is two-faced?

2. Can you remember a time when you were two-faced? If so, describe.

3. Would those who know you best describe your life as stable and integrous? If not, why?

4. Prayer for today: *Lord, give me a single heart for you.*

DAY 3 — QUESTIONS & Applications

1. Read James 3:1–12. What are these verses saying to you about how we use words?

2. In this passage of Scripture, which verse challenges you the most? Why?

3. Prayer for today: *Lord, may all my words come from a single heart.*

DAY 4 — QUESTIONS & Applications

1. Reflecting on James 3:9, have you ever blessed God and cursed (spoken against) people? Describe your experience.

2. When James said, "My brethren, these things ought not be this way" (James 3:10), what did he mean?

3. Prayer for today: *Lord, may my words be a blessing to you and others.*

DAY 5 — QUESTIONS & Applications

1. Read James 4:7–8. What are these verses saying to you?

2. Reflecting on James 4:8, what are some ways you can draw close to God?

3. Prayer for today: *Lord, I want to live as close to you as I can.*

DAY 6 — QUESTIONS & Applications

1. Read James 4:11 and James 5:9. What are these verses saying to you?

2. Have you ever spoken against or complained about someone? What was the effect of your words upon that person?

3. Prayer for today: *Lord, may my words be like fresh water to those around me.*

DAY 7 **QUESTIONS**
& Applications

1. Questions and Applications

2. Reflecting on this week, have you been unstable in your Christian witness? If so, why?

3. How can you live without ever being two-faced?

4. Prayer for today: *Lord, thank you for giving me a pure heart.*

LESSON 5

The Power of Negativity

While pastoring, I encountered an individual who, in my mind, possessed a PhD in negativity. No matter what I said, her response was always negative. One spring day, I complimented the beautiful flowers growing in her side flower bed. Her response was, "Yea, but I didn't have any come up on the other side of the house." I only remember seeing this individual laugh once in the years I pastored the church, but what I remember most is how her negativity shifted the atmosphere of the room.

Do you remember the Peanuts character, Pig-Pen? His name described what you saw. Everywhere Pig-Pen walked, a dust cloud hovered around his body. Negative people resemble this cartoon character because a depressing dust cloud follows them when they enter a room. Anyone within earshot of a negative person is sure to be covered with their gloomy words.

I remember chairing a meeting where the members were optimistically sharing ideas and plans were freely flowing concerning how our church would follow-up with first- time visitors, and then it happened; one team member began to gush negative verbiage about an experience he had as a visitor at a church. The laughter ceased, the atmosphere became heavy, ideas dwindled, and the meeting quickly ended. I later confronted that team member and brought correction, but the damage had already been done during the meeting to shift the atmosphere.

Studies have shown that negative words destroy more than atmospheres. A steady barrage of negativity can erode and ultimately destroy marriages, families, and children. Negative words are also detrimental on a large scale, causing destruction in organizations and businesses, not to mention churches. Research indicates that negative words can even be harmful to one's health.[3]

There are several reasons why a person might consistently speak negative words. Fear and unbelief are the reasons I want to underscore, and I believe they are two sides of the same coin. When we've lost sight of what God has said, our faith will diminish, and we are likely to begin speaking out of fear. When a person's reservoir is full of fear and not faith, their words will be tainted with negativity. Faith is seeing from God's perspective and placing trust in that reality. When our reality becomes greater in our minds than God's reality, we'll become overwhelmed by fear. At that point, our words will reflect the fear oppressing us.

This point is made abundantly clear in a story recorded in Numbers 13. The Lord told Moses that the land of Canaan belonged to the Israelites that and they only needed to possess it. Much like inspecting a new house before purchasing it, Israel was given an opportunity to explore their new territory. I can almost imagine God's excitement as He spoke with Moses about this land. He wanted this promised land of Canaan to be experienced by leaders and then the vision shared with His people. God desired the Israelites to look at this land as their possession, as their home.

Twelve spies were chosen to survey Canaan. When they came into the valley, they decided to bring a bit of the promised land back to the Israelites, so they cut off a single branch bearing a cluster of grapes. The grapes were so large that it required two men to carry the cluster suspended on a pole. Upon their return to the camp, they reported all that they had seen and then presented the fruit of the land. All looked well up to that point, but then they continued, "Nevertheless, the people who live in the land are strong, and the cities are fortified and very large" (Numbers 13:28a).

They proceeded to describe their enemies: the Hittites, Jebusites, Amorites, and Canaanites. Their report was so cloaked in fear that they described themselves as grasshoppers in the shadow of their enemies. Imagine the depth of their fear and despair. God's chosen people identifying themselves as small insignificant insects. This portrayal of themselves was a total disregard of who God said they were and what God had promised them.

Joshua and Caleb, however, gave a different report. These two men were flabbergasted by the negative report from the other ten spies, and they reminded the Israelites of God's promise. Yet, their faith was met with disdain. The Bible says that the other ten spies continued their negative chant, and even spread a "bad report" among Israel (Numbers 13:32). Their negative words spread like cancer throughout the entire Israelite nation, and it became so entrenched among the Israelites that they talked of stoning Joshua and Caleb for believing God's promise that they could possess the land.

The result was a forty-year delay before Israel entered the promised land. It must be stated that your negative words can hinder your company, church, ministry, or family. Words spoken out of unbelief and fear are usually negative, and they will rest on people like a shroud. After thirty years of pastoring, I can tell you how deadening negative words can be to a board or staff meeting. When someone speaks from a faithless position, their words scatter fear and dissension throughout an entire group of people.

So, let me give you three suggestions before you speak a word. First, don't speak when you are overwhelmed by circumstances. When surrounded by situations that you don't understand, wait, listen, and see what the Lord is saying before you speak. He is more aware of what's facing you than you are. It's best to speak only when He gives you words to say.

Second, don't speak when you are overpowered by critics. We tend to defend ourselves or our positions when we're faced with opposition. In those moments we're likely to allow our emotions to drive our words rather than the Spirit of God.

Third, don't speak when you are overcome by the crowds. Be careful not to allow popular opinion to drive your words. Crowds can be fickle, and people can get swept up in the tide of many voices screaming the same thing. Instead, listen for the still, small voice of the Lord. Trust His voice over popular voices around you.

Most of all, keep your eyes fixed on the Lord (see Hebrews 12:2). Learn to speak out of God's perspective. Allow faith to guide your words rather than fear and unbelief. May people be inspired by the words released from your mouth.

QUESTIONS

1. What has God promised you? Have you lost sight of those promises?

2. Are your words negative? Do you see problems over promises? If so, why?

3. What can you do to speak words of hope to the world around you?

> If you choose to extend this lesson for one week, then complete the following questions and applications each day.

DAY 2 — QUESTIONS & Applications

1. Read Numbers 13:1–27. What are your observations?

2. Did you observe anything in this passage that would cause fear?

3. Prayer for today: *Lord, make my words faith-filled.*

DAY 3 — QUESTIONS & Applications

1. Read Numbers 13:28–33. What are your observations?

2. In this passage of Scripture, what is the basis of their fear?

3. What are your observations of verse 32?

4. Prayer for today: *Lord, keep my eyes fixed on your promises.*

DAY 4 — QUESTIONS & Applications

1. Read Numbers 14:1–11. What are your observations?

2. How did negativity and fear affect the people of God?

3. What was the response from Joshua and Caleb?

4. Prayer for today: *Lord, help me trust you no matter what.*

DAY 5 — QUESTIONS & Applications

1. Reflecting on Numbers 13:1–33 and Numbers 14:1–11, what is God's response toward negativity, fear, and unbelief?

2. Have you ever witnessed negative attitudes hindering the plans of God? If so, explain.

3. Have you hindered God's plans because of negativity? If so, explain.

4. Prayer for today: *Lord, keep me from a negative mindset.*

DAY 6 — QUESTIONS & Applications

1. Can you identify two people in your life who are positive and filled with faith like Joshua and Caleb?

2. What enables a person to remain positive?

3. What are some ways you can maintain a positive perspective?

4. Prayer for today: *Lord, transform my attitude.*

DAY 7 QUESTIONS
& Applications

1. Reflecting on this week, have your words been full of faith or negative and faithless? Explain.

2. How has God spoken to you about the power of negativity?

3. What is your action plan to speak words of hope and faith to others?

4. Prayer for today: *Lord, thank you that my words are filled with hope.*

LESSON 6

Childish Christianity

Some of my most cherished moments, as a pastor, occurred when I had the privilege of walking a person through the prayer of confession of sin and for them to receive the redemptive power of Christ into their lives. In fact, the apex of all our decisions is to receive Christ as our Savior and Lord. One morning, I struck up a conversation with an employee serving at the hotel breakfast bar where I was staying. Soon our conversation turned toward Christ, and I encouraged her to attend services at the church where I was ministering. That evening she came and brought her family as well. At the end of the service, her entire family gave their lives to Christ. It was a blessed event to witness.

Yet, as much as I rejoice in witnessing a spiritual birth, I'm just as grieved by the lack of spiritual growth that seems so pervasive among believers. This stunted spiritual development has birthed many, many problems in the church, and it's not a new issue. The apostle Paul addressed spiritual immaturity in the church at Corinth.

Listen to his sobering rebuke, "And I, brethren, could not speak to you as to spiritual men, but as to men of flesh, as to infants in Christ. I gave you milk to drink, not solid food; for you were not yet able *to receive it.* Indeed, even now you are not yet able" (1 Corinthians 3:1–2). Paul wasn't addressing new believers but those who had never matured in their spiritual lives. Therefore, he called them infants (*nepios*), a term that refers to childish believers.

Paul had to reduce his teaching menu to elementary lessons. Much like giving a bottle to a baby, these believers couldn't handle solid truths. So, they were given milk to drink—a metaphor indicating their immaturity. Paul described their childish behavior as the root of the jealousy and strife within the church. Strife (*eris*) means division that occurs through arguing, contention, and debating. The church at Corinth was fractured and splintered because immature believers allowed their mouths to become a source of dissention.

Immature Christians create spiritual chaos. They use words with little concern regarding their impact or damage. They won't take responsibility for what they say; instead, they place blame on others. They deflect, defend, debate, and sow discord among other believers. Sadly, I've observed people worship with their hands held high in the air and then, in their selfish immaturity, make stinging comments about someone in the same congregation only moments after the service. I've watched churches fragment and divide because contentious words were spoken or even posted on Facebook. Like small children, immature believers create messes in families, at work, and within churches.

As a parent and now a grandparent, I expect babies and small children to be messy. No one blushes when a baby spits up. No one thinks it's strange when a twelve-month old dirties its diaper. Not only do we anticipate those things happening, but we also prepare for them. We've all lugged bags full of wipes, burp cloths, and diapers. The immaturity of infants is expected, but when immaturity manifests through a believer who should know better, it's insufferable. Stinking messes made by childish believers, especially with their mouths, has caused irreparable damage within the body of Christ.

In Proverbs 6:16–19, the Bible identifies seven things that are an abomination to God. These are so disgusting it makes Him nauseous. The last item on this list refers to a person who spreads strife among the body of Christ. God is sick to His stomach when immature believers verbally instigate strife among their spiritual brothers and sisters. The word strife (*medan*) is derived from a Hebrew word that means to cause discord. It's a picture of someone who spreads seeds of disunity within groups of people.

The way you speak to people or about them reflects your spiritual maturity. Families, small groups, employees, or church congregations should become more unified by your influence. If your words sow division, dissention, and discord wherever you go, maybe it's time to grow up. It's no grand secret that spiritual maturity is both a process of time and an application of spiritual disciplines. While we can't rush time, let me suggest several disciplines you can apply. First, acknowledge your own childish Christian experience. Own up to your messes, admit when your wrong, and confess your immaturity to God. Confession is the first place to begin.

Second, regularly consume the Word of God. Your diet must change if you expect to grow and speak words of life. Truly, you are what you eat. You will always remain spiritually malnourished if you consistently fill your mind and heart with things like media, news, Facebook, TV, office chatter, and disparaging reports. I'm not suggesting we ignore the world; just don't love the things of the world (see 1 John 2:15). Love the truth of God's Word. Allow the Scriptures to wash over you (see Ephesians 5:26). A steady diet of the Word and its application will place you on the track of spiritual growth.

Third, consistent prayer. The Bible instructs us to pray without ceasing (1 Thessalonians 5:17). That would mean at any moment in our day, we are engaged in prayer. How is that possible? Obviously, prayer is more than us talking to God. Effective prayer is listening more than speaking. To pray without ceasing means to remain in constant communion with God. In other words, our hearts should remain connected to Him every moment of our day. We're never to be out of touch with our heavenly Father.

Prayer, then, becomes as natural and consistent as breathing. Our spirit is communing with the Spirit of God, and we're engaged in a posture of listening, ready to think, act, or speak under God's prompting. By listening to God, speaking with God, and obeying every leading from God, your mouth will become a wellspring of life. Living in this manner will cause us to grow up much sooner than later, and our words will most likely not intentionally cause dissension and division.

QUESTIONS

1. Do your words cause unity or divisions among people? (Take inventory over the last ten years of your life and all the people you have associated with and be honest).

2. Are you spiritually mature or immature? How can you discern the difference?

3. How can you use words to be a blessing to people around you?

If you choose to extend this lesson for one week, then complete the following questions and applications each day.

DAY 2 — QUESTIONS & Applications

1. Read 1 Corinthians 1:10. What are your observations of this verse?

2. Read 1 Corinthians 3:1–5. What are your observations?

3. Prayer for today: *Lord, don't let me speak divisive words.*

DAY 3   QUESTIONS & Applications

1. Reflecting on 1 Corinthians 3:1, what did Paul mean when he addressed his audience as "brethren"?

2. Reflecting on 1 Corinthians 3:1 (NASB), Paul described his audience as men of flesh. What does that mean?

3. Prayer for today: *Lord, keep me from speaking in the flesh.*

DAY 4   QUESTIONS & Applications

1. Reflecting on 1 Corinthians 3:3–4, what are the negative fruits of spiritual immaturity?

2. Read Proverbs 6:16–19. What are your observations? Why do you believe these seven things are so disgusting to God?

3. Prayer for today: *Lord, may my words bring joy to you.*

DAY 5   QUESTIONS
& Applications

1. Reflecting on Proverbs 6:16–19, is the Lord disgusted with anything in your life? If so, what? How will you change?

2. Read 1 Corinthians 11:17–18. What are your observations?

3. Prayer for today: *Lord, may my words unite people, not divide them.*

DAY 6   QUESTIONS
& Applications

1. Define what you believe to be spiritual maturity. Where are you on that spectrum?

2. How would living spiritually mature be reflected in the words you use? In difficult relationships?

3. Based on the words you speak, do they indicate that you are spiritually growing? Explain.

4. Prayer for today: *Lord, let my words reflect the nature of Christ.*

DAY 7

QUESTIONS
& Applications

1. Reflecting on this week, have your words been divisive or unifying? Explain.

2. Review the three ways a person can spiritually grow: confession of immaturity, consuming the Word, and consistent prayer. Have you implemented these into your life? Which one has been most helpful? Why?

3. What are some other ways you can mature spiritually?

4. Prayer for today: *Lord, may I grow up in Christ.*

LESSON 7

Challenging Circumstances

In 2005, Canadian singer, Daniel Powter released the pop song, *Bad Day*. Powter recorded the song in 2002, but due to extenuating circumstances, it's release was delayed. The song title says it all: sometimes life presents us with a bad day. We all have days where bad things happen, but there are those who have challenging days that turn into weeks, months, and even years. Some don't triumph through adverse circumstances very well, and there are those who seem to prevail through peril. It's those who navigate through perplexing situations and still maintain a victorious attitude without complaining that inspire me most.

At the top of the list would be the apostle Paul. After completing his last missionary journey, he went to Jerusalem to share his experiences. The Jews, however, were not pleased with Paul because he ministered to Gentiles. Consequently, they searched for any accusation they could launch at him. Paul entered the temple at the urging of his companions to complete a ceremonial cleansing—mostly to appease the Jews. They seized the opportunity and accused Paul of violating the law by bringing a Greek into the temple.

In moments, the city erupted, and they dragged Paul out of the temple and proceeded to beat him. He was spared momentarily by Roman soldiers, but when Paul reported to the Jews that he had been commissioned by God to minister to Gentiles, they made an oath not to eat or drink until they killed him. Paul escaped with his life because four hundred and seventy Roman soldiers decided to escort him to Caesarea to evade the angry mob. Paul spent another two years in custody pleading his innocence as a lawbreaker but to no avail. Finally, he requested to stand before Caesar in Rome hoping to be set free.

The trip to Rome was just as challenging including storms, shipwreck, snake bite, and being forced to spend the winter on the island of Malta. Finally arriving in Rome, Paul found himself bound and placed on house arrest for another two years. During this arrest, he was chained twenty-four/seven to one of Caesar's guards. While in prison, Paul's critics took the opportunity to denigrate his character and ministry. It was during this period, several years after being escorted out of Jerusalem by Roman soldiers, that Paul wrote a letter to believers in Philippi about his circumstances (see Philippians 1:12). Can you imagine what Paul could have reported?

Put yourself in his sandals. You have waited over four years for someone to hear the truth about your life. And while you wait, still in custody, people continue to criticize you, your character, and your ministry. How easy would it be to complain about your circumstances, how life isn't fair, or how you've been mistreated?

If we are honest, complaining is a way of life for so many. We complain about the weather, sports, politics, our jobs, and the price of gas. We are daily inundated with people's complaints and grumbling about their circumstances. How would that verbal diet influence the way we would handle what Paul endured? His life was a series of bad days . . . bad months . . . bad years.

Not a single word of complaint came out of Paul's mouth. In fact, note what he wrote to the believers in Philippi, "Do everything without grumbling or disputing" (Philippians 2:14a). The Passion Translation states it this way: "Live a cheerful life, without complaining or division among yourselves. For then you will be seen as innocent, faultless, and pure children of God, even though you live amid brutal and perverse culture. For you will appear among them as shining lights in the universe, offering them the words of eternal life" (Philippians 2:14–16a).

How do we become shining lights in our universe? By living cheerful lives that are free of complaints regardless the challenging circumstances in which we find ourselves. Complaining is the way of the world, but rejoicing is the way of the kingdom. Refusing to complain indicates that Christ *in* you is greater than what is happening *to* you.

Despite Paul's circumstances, he said things like "always offering prayer with joy" (Philippians 1:4), "my circumstances have turned out for the greater progress of the gospel" (Philippians 1:12), "in this I will rejoice" (Philippians 1:18), and "in no way alarmed by opponents" (Philippians 1:28). Paul's refusal to gripe and complain about his circumstances ultimately impacted those chained to him. The whole praetorian guard learned the truth about Christ because Paul didn't complain to them. Each rotation of soldiers found themselves face-to-face with a man who talked about the gospel instead of his miserable circumstances (see Philippians 1:12–13).

Some scholars point out that the praetorian guards were nine thousand of the finest, seasoned soldiers, and every four hours there was a guard change. That meant that over a period of two years, Paul potentially had the opportunity to influence 4,220 men. Paul closed his letter with, "All the saints greet you, especially those in Caesar's household" (Philippians 4:22). How did saints get into Caesar's household? Because one man spoke about Christ to Caesar's guards rather than lamenting and complaining about his circumstances.

I don't mean to trivialize the difficulties you face right now. You may be surrounded by emotional, relational, physical, and financial situations that seem unbearable. Maybe you feel like you've been bound and chained to these circumstances for months or even years. Believe it or not, this could be one of the greatest moments in your life to advance the cause for Christ if you learn to endure without complaining. How can you keep from speaking complaints? Let me suggest five words: recognize, repent, realize, relinquish, and rejoice.

Recognize that complaining is part of your regular conversation. *Repent* and change your perspective about your circumstances and confess your need of God's grace. *Realize* that what you're going through hasn't surprised God. In fact, He will work all your challenges together and bring something good from them (see Romans 8:28). *Relinquish* all lies that you have agreed with such as: my life is a failure, this will never change, I will never be free from this, or I am a bad parent. Don't allow the enemy to badger you into believing things that contradict the truth of God's Word. Finally, *rejoice* no matter what you're going through. Let your mouth become an instrument of praise (see 1 Thessalonians 5:18).

These changes will be challenging, but remember that you are in excellent company, considering the life of Paul. Over time you can cease from all complaining—no matter what you're going through. More importantly, God will use your circumstances to advance the cause of the gospel.

QUESTIONS

1. What are some challenging circumstances that you are in? How are you coping?

2. Would your family or friends say you complain or rejoice while in a conflict?

3. What are some steps you can take that will help you rejoice through difficult circumstances?

If you choose to extend this lesson for one week, then complete the following questions and applications each day.

DAY 2 — QUESTIONS & Applications

1. The history of Paul's circumstances explored in this lesson is found in Acts chapters 21–28. It's lengthy, so you may want to spend this week reading those chapters. They will give you a biblical understanding of Paul's circumstances.

2. Why do you believe people complain? Why do some people *not* complain?

3. Prayer for today: *Lord, keep me from complaining.*

DAY 3 — QUESTIONS & Applications

1. Read Philippians 4:4–8. (Keep in mind that Paul wrote the book of Philippians while on house arrest and bound to a guard.) What are your observations?

2. Reflecting on these verses, what are some steps to keep you from complaining?

3. Prayer for today: *Lord, my mind will be filled with the right stuff.*

DAY 4 — QUESTIONS & Applications

1. Read Philippians 3:12–14. What are your observations?

2. Reflecting on these verses, how can they keep you from complaining?

3. Prayer for today: *Lord, help me to keep my eyes on you.*

DAY 5   QUESTIONS
& Applications

1. Read Philippians 1:15–20. What are your observations?

2. What was Paul's attitude toward his critics? How can you respond like Paul did?

3. Prayer for today: *Lord, enable me to love those who mistreat me.*

DAY 6   QUESTIONS
& Applications

1. Review the five ways to cease from complaining: recognize, repent, realize, relinquish, and rejoice. Which one challenges you most? Explain.

2. Read Roman 8:28. What are your observations?

3. Prayer for today: *Lord, I will trust you no matter the circumstances.*

DAY 7   QUESTIONS
& Applications

1. Reflecting on this week, have you ceased from complaining? Explain how/when/where.

2. What are your actions steps to live without speaking any complaints?

3. Read 1 Thessalonians 5:18. Ask the Lord to make this verse true in your life.

4. Prayer for today: *Lord, I will always rejoice, no matter what happens.*

LESSON 8

No More Gossip

A study conducted at the University of Arizona found that most people use approximately 16,000 words per day. This same study also debunked the common myth that women speak more words than men. Of course, it was determined that the number of words spoken each day is contingent upon the type of career one has, but in the final analysis men and woman speak approximately the same number of words each day. With that being said, we must ask ourselves how many of our words are necessary, and if they are necessary, are they beneficial to hearers?

The writer of Proverbs warned, "When there are many words, transgression is unavoidable, but he who restrains his lips is wise" (Proverbs 10:19). The New Living Translation states it this way: "Too much talk leads to sin. Be sensible and keep your mouth shut." When words are plentiful, it leads to flattery, exaggeration, inauthenticity, deception, and arguments. Additionally, in the needless gush of words, we run the risk of gossip.

I read recently that gossip is speaking to someone who is not directly part of the problem or part of the solution, about another person who is not present, but who is a participant in the situation. If I'm in conflict with a person, I must not bring others into this conflict. Otherwise, I am talking behind someone's back to use the adage. It's one thing to honor someone who isn't present in the conversation, but to speak negatively or gossip is entirely different. It's slanderous in nature and can destroy the reputation of other individuals.

The apostle Paul expressed his concern about gossip when he wrote, "For I am afraid that perhaps when I come I may find you to be not what I wish and . . . that perhaps there will be strife, jealousy, angry tempers, disputes, slanders, [and] gossip . . ." (2 Corinthians 12:20a). This is a sobering list of problems and obviously several issues resulting from speaking needless words, but let's explore gossip.

This specific word for gossip (*psithurismos*) is only used here in the New Testament. It means to whisper secrets, to give a malicious report about another person. It's derived from the Hebrew word "charmed" in Ecclesiastes 10:11. This word carries the idea of speaking incantations or invoking the demonic, much like divination. Gossip, then, is more than secretly passing on information about another person; it summons the enemy into our conversations.

In 2 Timothy 3:3, Paul used the words "malicious gossips." They are derived from the Greek word *diabolos*, which is the word for devil. When we gossip about another person, we are destroying the character of another in the same manner as the devil would. Perhaps we're never more like the enemy than when we gossip about people and pass on hurtful information to others.

Now we can begin to understand why Paul was so fearful that he would find the Corinthian believers not as he wished. He knew if they gossiped about each other, that they were inviting the enemy to wreak havoc within their community life. Painfully, I've watched congregations disintegrate because of gossip. In Paul's first letter to the Corinthians, he addressed problems such as disunity, factions, and divisions, which are the fruit of gossip. If you think for one second that you can share hurtful information about another person without any fallout, then you are deceived. Over my years of ministry, I've ministered to many people who have been victims of gossip. Their wounds are deep and wide.

Years ago, I remember playing a game with a group of twenty-five people. One person began the game by sharing a silly, easily repeated, thirty-second story with the person next to them. The story was whispered and retold over and over as it traveled around the circle. At last, the tale arrived back to the person who began the story. The first and the last storyteller compared their story, and interestingly, the stories didn't match. We repeated the game, with heightened attentiveness, and we found the same results. The changes subtly occurred with each exchange.

This game demonstrated how information was distorted as it was exchanged between people. The same results occur when we pass on information about other people. Facts are embellished, and the truth is lost as it travels from one person to the next. And worse still, the enemy uses gossipers as pawns, but gossip is no game. As believers, we simply cannot allow ourselves to get caught up in trafficking unnecessary verbiage about other people. You must make the declaration that there will be no more gossip in your life.

How do you prevent being a part of gossip? Let me give you several suggestions. First, ask yourself if the conversation you are having with another person is gossip. Are you speaking to someone who is neither directly part of the problem or part of the solution, concerning another person who is not present? Second, if you discover that you are, then be bold enough to stop speaking about the other person. You might say, "Truthfully, I don't believe we should be speaking negatively about this person."

The third suggestion is to become the person's ally by offering to pray for them. When I was pastoring, if someone shared unnecessary information with me about someone else, I would suggest that we pray for the person. So, when unkind or ill information surfaced in our conversation about another person, I would gently end the conversation and say, "Let's take a moment to pray for this person." Not only did we bless the person who was needlessly brought into the conversation, but simultaneously, it was made clear to the person whom I was conversing with that gossip would not be tolerated. This action usually ended any future attempts for this person to bring me into their gossip.

Finally, at the end of each day, simply ask the Holy Spirit if you misrepresented anyone with your words. May we be people who never gossip about others.

QUESTIONS

1. Have you ever participated in gossip? Are you willing to repent of this sin?

2. Have you witnessed the effects of gossip? If so, where and what were the effects?

3. Will you commit to submitting an inventory of your words to the scrutiny of the Holy Spirit at the end of each day?

4. Will you actively utilize the plan outlined above to halt your participation in gossip?

> If you choose to extend this lesson for one week, then complete the following questions and applications each day.

DAY 2 — QUESTIONS & Applications

1. Read 2 Corinthians 12:20. What are your observations on this verse?

2. Reflecting on this verse, what problems do you see because of gossip?

3. In the NASB, Paul listed slander as one of his concerns. Is there a difference between gossip and slander? Explain.

4. Prayer for today: *Lord, steer me away from gossip.*

DAY 3 QUESTIONS
& Applications

1. Read Romans 1:29–30 and 2 Timothy 3:1–3. What are your observations of these passages?

2. Reflecting on these two passages, did you note "gossip" in the verses? What are other problems related to gossip that you observed?

3. Prayer for today: *Lord, may I honor others when I speak.*

DAY 4 QUESTIONS
& Applications

1. Read Proverbs 10:19. Why do you think transgression is unavoidable with many words?

2. Are all your words throughout the day necessary? How can you limit unnecessary words from your life?

3. Prayer for today: *Lord, enable me to speak only necessary words.*

DAY 5   QUESTIONS
& Applications

1. Have you ever ended a conversation because of gossip? Do you have the courage to do so? If so, how will you do it?

2. Have you ever sincerely prayed for someone who shouldn't have come up in your conversation? If so, did it help to end gossip?

3. Have you ever sensed an evil presence when you heard gossip? If so, explain.

4. Prayer for today: *Lord, I will take action against gossiping.*

DAY 6   QUESTIONS
& Applications

1. Do you believe it is easy for people to gossip? If so, why?

2. What benefit do people think is derived from gossiping?

3. Do you believe the enemy is attracted to gossip? If so, why?

4. Prayer for today: *Lord, I will bless others with my words.*

DAY 7

QUESTIONS
& Applications

1. Reflecting on this week, have you kept from gossiping? Explain.

2. What are some actions steps that the Holy Spirit has given you to prevent gossip?

3. Prayer for today: *Lord, I am free from speaking badly about others.*

LESSON 9

Angry Words

Recently, I read that people are angrier today than they were several decades ago. I'm not sure if that is true, but it can be argued that there are more platforms for people to vent their anger. Facebook, for example, has become one such forum for unbridled venomous words.

Research is mixed regarding the sources of anger and its possible value. Many psychologists identify trigger events as the source and point out that the degree of anger is usually linked to personality traits. For example, someone who is a perfectionist, research says, may react to chaos with a greater degree of frustration than someone with an easy-going temperament. Other researchers believe anger is the second emotion, triggered by hurt, the repressed first emotion. Most people disdain feeling vulnerable when they have been hurt, but anger allows people to *feel* a sense of control.

As for the value of anger, does it really motivate us to do good? Perhaps if a person is angry over injustice, such as child abuse, then their provocation may prompt them into action. As believers, should we become angry? The real issue for a believer is what we permit to motivate us. Anger itself is an emotion much like fear, excitement, or being nervous. While emotions are amoral, they cannot become the source for our actions. As Christians, we must be sourced by the Holy Spirit (see Galatians 5:25).

For example, Jesus was angry with the religious leaders in Mark 3:5. Their adherence to the Law led them to overlook the needs of a crippled man. In fact, some expositors suggest that they exploited a crippled man only to bring accusations against Jesus; therefore, they had no regard for his individual value or needs. Surrounded by such carnal attitudes and hardness of heart, Jesus was stirred with anger toward the Pharisees. Yet, He never spoke with harsh words or acted in a vindictive manner because of anger. He was sourced only by the Father, not emotions (see John 5:19 and 12:49).

James stated, ". . . Everyone must be quick to hear, slow to speak *and* slow to anger; for the anger of man does not achieve the righteousness of God" (James 1:19–20). Anger may not be a sin, but it doesn't produce or bring forth the righteousness of God. Therefore, James admonished us to be slow, sluggish, not hasty to anger. The emotion of anger can overtake our sensitivity and compliance to the Holy Spirit, and we'll become motivated purely out of anger. In other words, anger becomes the source of our words and actions rather than God. When that happens, we will not achieve the righteousness of God.

Paul stated, "Be angry, and *yet* do not sin; do not let the sun go down on your anger, and do not give the devil an opportunity" (Ephesians 4:26). A simpler translation is, "While in your anger, do not sin." This is not a command advocating anger, but it admonishes us not to sin when anger is present. Paul then stated another command to resolve anger as soon as possible; otherwise, lingering anger can give the enemy an opportunity—giving him space to function—in your life.

Anger (*orge*) carries the idea of being provoked with violent passion or to be deeply moved with fury. Actions discharged under those unbridled conditions can be very hurtful to others. It's interesting to note that within the same context of Paul's exhortation about anger, he addressed speaking unwholesome words and grieving the Spirit, which are two probabilities that can occur with unresolved anger (Ephesians 4:29–30). In a state of anger, we're likely to speak harshly, critically, and even brutally. Wounding other people with angry words is certainly one way to grieve the Holy Spirit.

This word for anger also means to punish, meaning we're so angry with someone that we desire for them to be punished. We may not hurt the person physically, but we might resort to inflicting pain with our words. Sometimes this is disguised as jokes, sarcasm, and mild insults. I was part of a church staff meeting one time and heard some comments made toward leadership that revealed buried anger. The remarks were not direct, but they were laced with enough cynicism that I and a few others could discern problems just below the surface.

How do we defuse anger appropriately? Paul wrote, "Let all bitterness and wrath and anger and clamor and slander be put away from you, along with all malice" (Ephesians 4:31). The verb put away (*airo*) means to remove, take, eliminate, destroy, or terminate. Because the verb is passive, it tells us that we're being acted upon, meaning Christ is the One who does the work through us. Left to our own efforts, anger can become very destructive. We must solicit the help of the Lord if we desire to be free from the sting and consequences of anger.

of sinning in our anger

Paul concluded by stating we must forgive others just as Christ has forgiven us (Ephesians 4:32). Forgiveness is the only way to remain free from long-term anger. When we truly forgive, we are choosing to grant favor upon the person we've been provoked with. The grace and favor we extend to someone are given regardless of their deserving it. When Christ forgave us, He extended grace to our lives even though we were undeserving.

If you discover that you've been provoked or angered by something you believe is injustice, like child abuse, pornography, abortion, or spiritual apathy, then ask yourself three questions before you utter a word. First, is this the time to speak? Perhaps waiting to release words during your agitation would be prudent. Remember James' exhortation to be slow to speak (James 1:19). This also allows time for the Holy Spirit to correct or align your heart and emotions to His.

Second, is this the way to speak? The tone and manner in which you speak is crucial to your integrity as a believer. Proverbs 15:1 says, "A gentle answer turns away wrath, but a harsh word stirs up anger." Regardless of your feelings of agitation, the Lord will enable you to speak with kind words. There is no occasion for believers to be rude, abrasive, or cruel when speaking to others.

Third, is this the person who needs to hear it? Innocent bystanders should not become the sounding board for your irritation. If you have been provoked by something, then take time to pray about it first. Speak to the Lord about the situation before you speak to anyone else.

May today be the start of never speaking angry words.

QUESTIONS

1. Are you angry about something? If so, what is the source of it?

2. What are some ways you have learned to diffuse anger? Are they Christ-like ways or flesh outlets?

3. Have you resolved all conflict with others? If not, why?

If you choose to extend this lesson for one week, then complete the following questions and applications each day.

DAY 2

QUESTIONS
& Applications

1. Do you believe anger is a valuable emotion? Explain.

2. Are there "just causes" that motivate your anger?

3. How do you believe Jesus dealt with His anger in Mark 3:5?

4. Prayer for today: *Lord, may I be Spirit led and not led emotionally.*

DAY 3 QUESTIONS
& Applications

1. Read James 1:19–20. What are your observations?

2. Read Ephesians 4:25–31. Concerning the topic of anger, what are your observations?

3. Prayer for today: *Lord, instruct me about the emotion of anger.*

DAY 4 QUESTIONS
& Applications

1. Read Luke 6:20–31 and 17:1–4. What are your observations of these passages?

2. Concerning the passages above, how did Jesus suggest diffusing anger?

3. Prayer for today: *Lord, enable me to follow your commands.*

DAY 5 — QUESTIONS & Applications

1. How do you respond when someone expresses angry words toward you?

2. How can a person be angry and not sin?

3. Read Proverbs 15:1. How does gentleness turn away wrath? Are you gentle with others?

4. Prayer for today: *Lord, enable me to be gentle in every situation.*

DAY 6 — QUESTIONS & Applications

1. Read Proverbs 16:32. What are your observations?

2. James 1:20 states that anger doesn't achieve the righteousness of God. Why do you believe this Scripture is true?

3. Is there ever a time when anger *does* achieve the righteousness of God? If so, explain.

4. Prayer for today: *Lord, govern all my emotions today.*

DAY 7   QUESTIONS
& Applications

1. Reflecting on this week, in volatile situations, have you spoken without angry words? Explain.

2. What are some lessons the Holy Spirit has taught you this week about anger?

3. What are some practical ways you will live without anger sourcing your words?

4. Prayer for today: *Lord, thank you that anger will not source my words.*

LESSON 10

Truth about Lies

The *Merriam-Webster Dictionary* defines lying as "to make an untrue statement with the intent to deceive." The operative word is the *intent* to deceive. Lying is not mistaken information. If I gave you incorrect directions, that wouldn't be classified as lying because my intentions would not be centered on deception.

Lying, then, is for the purpose of intentionally deceiving another person. People lie to gain a strategic advantage over someone else. Others lie because they desire to avoid punishment or don't want to disappoint someone. Still, others lie to gain approval or to win admiration. No matter the reason, lying is wrong and associated with the father of lies—Satan (see John 8:44).

Lying generally falls into four categories. First, fabrication, which is a blatant, willful deception. Often it finds roots at an early age. Years ago, the young boy who lived next door threw a rock at one of my sons. When I asked him why he did it, he told me the rock slipped out of his hands as he was polishing it. That was the best that he could come up with.

Second, exaggeration. This is the amplification of the truth to make something bigger or better than it really is. Pastors, unfortunately, are notorious for this; I know because I used to do it. How many did you have on Easter Sunday? "Standing room only," was my answer, and, of course, that was in the hallway. Though this sounds innocent, exaggerating a story is still a form of deception, and it is wrong.

Third, minimization. This is diminishing the truth so that it doesn't appear as bad as it really is. The first time I wrecked my father's car on an icy road, I spun-out and slid into someone's front yard. I not only damaged the car and several mailboxes, but I leveled a few small trees and left large ruts in the front yard. I managed to get the car out of the yard and safely back home. I told my father the car slipped a little bit on the ice. That was a massive understatement, and it didn't hold up when he inspected the car the next day.

Fourth, omission. In this category, we know what the truth is, but we choose to omit it from our story. Not sharing the truth when it's sincerely sought is a form of deception. Cindy and I have agreed in our marriage that if the truth is sought, the truth will be heard. That even includes sensitive topics such as, does this outfit look good? Yep, if truth is required, then truth must be spoken. But we've also learned to do so in love according to Ephesians 4:15. Truth should not be used as a weapon, which is why love must deliver the truth.

Lying, no matter the category, is wrong, and the Bible has strong statements about it. God hates lying lips (Proverbs 6:17), and "lying lips are an abomination to the Lord" (Proverbs 12:22). Whoever pours out lies, the Bible says, will perish (Proverbs 19:9). Revelation 21:8 lists sins that are worthy of the lake of fire, and one of those sins is lying. The psalmist cried out to be delivered from lying and deceitfulness, and Paul wrote that since we've laid aside our old selves, we should not lie to one another.

In 1 Peter 2:21, the Bible says Christ is the supreme example whom we should follow. In verse 22, we read that Jesus committed no sin and there wasn't any deceit in His mouth. May it be said of us that there is no deceit in our mouths.

One of the most profound statements about truth-telling says, "Therefore, laying aside falsehood, speak truth each one of you with his neighbor" (Ephesians 4:25). Falsehood (*pseudos*) is derived from a word that means counterfeit. Something that is counterfeit is forgery; it imitates something that is real with the intent to deceive. Some estimate that there are 60 to 80 million U.S. dollars in counterfeit money circulating and adversely affecting the economy. Just imagine, however, the way counterfeit Christianity effects the cause of Christ.

Some scholars liken falsehood to the fig leaves Adam sewed for coverings in Genesis 3:7. Adam and Eve hid themselves from the presence of God because of guilt and shame. Their fig leaves covered more than their nakedness; it was an attempt to disguise their sin. Many years later, Christians still hide behind their masks because of guilt and shame. Believers settle for *pseudo* community unable to unveil their falsehood and expose their sin, which is how healing transpires (see James 5:16). The apostle Paul argued for an authentic body of Christ where members remove facades, uncover sin, and speak honestly to each other.

A similar word to *pseudos* was used in Matthew 23:13 by Jesus to describe the Scribes and Pharisees. He said they were hypocrites (*hupokrites*), a compound word that means to speak or act under a false part. The religious leaders of Jesus' day *pretended* to be religious mentors, but their hypocrisy and in-authenticity kept people from entering the kingdom of heaven. Jesus confronted them for their *pseudo* religious practices, stating that they were done in pretense. He called them white-washed tombs who appeared beautiful on the outside but were full of dead bones on the inside (Matthew 23:27).

Paul continued in Ephesians by exhorting believers to imitate God through a life of love and to avoid immorality, impurity, greed, filthiness, silly talk, and coarse jesting (Ephesians 5:1–4). Paul admonishes us to "walk as children of Light" (Ephesians 5:8). Light exposes what is in the darkness. Usually, one cannot hide very well in the light. By walking in the Light, Paul was underscoring the necessity to lay aside all falsehood and live, act, and speak authentically.

John made a similar statement when he said, "This is the message we have heard from Him and announce to you, that God is Light, and in Him there is no darkness at all" (1 John 1:5). When we consistently walk in the Light, John said, our sin is cleansed. With sin removed, we're enabled to live and speak without deception.

Let's learn to live and speak the truth.

QUESTIONS

1. Are you a person who speaks deceit? If so, why?

2. Why do you believe speaking honestly and truthfully is difficult for people? What discoveries about lying have you found in the Bible?

3. What are ways that you can start to speak the truth in love?

If you choose to extend this lesson for one week, then complete the following questions and applications each day.

DAY 2

QUESTIONS
& Applications

1. Reflect on the four categories of lying: fabrication, exaggeration, minimization, and omission. Have you fallen prey to any of these forms of deception? If so, explain.

2. Why do people tell lies? Why have you told lies before?

3. Prayer for today: *Lord, empower me to be a truth-teller.*

DAY 3   QUESTIONS
& Applications

1. Review the following Scriptures: Proverbs 6:16–19, Proverbs 12:19 and 22, Proverbs 19:5 and 9, Proverbs 24:28, Proverbs 25:18. What are your observations?

2. Read 1 Peter 2:21–22. What are your observations?

3. Prayer for today: *Lord, enable me to be just like you in what I say.*

DAY 4   QUESTIONS
& Applications

1. Read Ephesians 4:25. What are your observations?

2. Do you believe people easily hide behind masks? Explain.

3. How did Adam and Eve respond when confronted by the truth? (see Genesis 3:8–13).

4. Prayer for today: *Lord, help me to speak authentic.*

DAY 5 — QUESTIONS & Applications

1. Have you ever been caught in a lie? If so, what happened?

2. Were the Pharisees of Jesus' day liars? (see Matthew 23:13). What are some ways to describe a hypocrite?

3. Prayer for today: *Lord, don't ever let me pretend to be spiritual.*

DAY 6 — QUESTIONS & Applications

1. Read Ephesians 5:8. What do you think it means to walk as children of light?

2. Read 1 John 1:5. What are your observations?

3. Prayer for today: *Lord, today I will walk as light.*

DAY 7

QUESTIONS
& Applications

1. Reflecting on this week, have you spoken any lies? Explain.

2. What are some key points the Holy Spirit has taught you this week about deception?

3. What is your plan to always speak the truth?

4. Prayer for today: *Lord, I will live and speak the truth.*

LESSON 11

Bridle the Tongue

I had the privilege to ride a 2,000-pound Haflinger-Belgium horse named JJ. The raw power of this animal was quite intimidating. The owner cautioned me not to let him sense my fear. If I'm calm, then the horse is calm . . . simple as that, right? I remained calm, but this massive horse still wanted to test my resolve. But I'm pleased to report that at the end of the day, I was able to lead the horse where I wanted to go. The secret, beyond being broken and trained for riding, is a small piece of metal in the mouth of the horse called a bit. Without the bit, someone like me with little training wouldn't be able to control an animal that size.

James 1:26 says, "If anyone thinks himself to be religious, and yet does not bridle his tongue but deceives his own heart, this man's religion is worthless." The term bridle (*chalinago-geo*) means to control, restrain, restrict, or subdue something. James is the only biblical author to use the imagery of reins, or the bridle, in relationship with the tongue. With little surprise then, we see how he wrote so plainly about an unbridled tongue, such as it makes great boasts (James 3:5), it sets things on fire (James 3:6), it defiles the body (James 3:6), it is full of deadly poison (James 3:8), and it curses people (James 3:9).

The inability to control our tongues results in reckless, dangerous, and hurtful words. Like an unrestrained animal, speaking with no constraint will cause enormous damage both in our lives and the lives of others. Additionally, James indicated how speaking with an unbridled tongue is evidence that we're deceiving ourselves. We believe that we're pious when our religion is worthless. The Passion Translation of James 1:26 says it this way: "If someone believes they have a relationship with God but fails to guard his words then his heart is drifting away and his religion is shallow and empty."

Devotion to God is in question, in other words, when we cannot bridle something as small as our tongue. James addressed how small things have a large effect, like a massive forest being set aflame by a small fire—perhaps nothing more than a spark. He wrote about a massive ship on the sea piloted by a small rudder. He referred to a horse—perhaps one the size of JJ—that is guided by a small bit in its mouth. And he said the tongue being so very small can make great boasts.

An adult tongue weighs no more than 70 grams (that's 0.15 pounds). Yet, according to James, this small part can "defile" the entire body (James 3:6). Defile means to place a stain over our entire life and reputation. One simple word spoken in haste or with the wrong tone, or a word filled with deception, judgment, or anger, can have a detrimental effect on our spiritual witness. Even more, unbridled words can destroy organizations or steer churches off course.

I remember observing a growing church nearly capsize when a member spoke harshly toward another member and then refused to make amends. One unbridled word led to another, and then one family spoke with unrestrained words toward another family. Reckless, untamed words about others were not only released in private settings but posted on Facebook for all to see. This caused irreconcilable damaged in the congregation, and these families eventually left the church because they were unable to worship together in a Spirit of unity.

James said the tongue is a "restless evil and full of deadly poison" (James 3:8b). Poison (*ios*) is the word describing venom secreted from a snake's mouth. A snake's venom usually targets a person's heart, muscles, or brain, and without immediate attention a human being will die. Perhaps James had in mind the crafty words the serpent enticed Eve with that led to mankind's destruction and death (see 2 Corinthians 11:3). Maybe he pondered quarrels and conflicts among people that have led to death (see James 4:1–2). Relationships simply will not survive the poison of an unbridled tongue unless intervention occurs.

James continued to describe the tongue as being restless (*akatastatos*), a word that means unstable, disorderly, and uncontrollable. "For every species of beasts and birds, of reptiles and creatures of the sea, is tamed and has been tamed by the human race. But no one can tame the tongue" (James 3:7–8a). What hope do we have against a small but restless and uncontrollable tongue that is full of deadly poison as James described?

I've heard all the excuses too. People will tell me, "That's just the way we talk at work," "That's my personality," "I wouldn't have said anything if they hadn't made me mad," "I have my rights," "I'm speaking my mind," and on and on it goes. Our small tongue continues to defile and destroy our reputation and ruin the lives of others around us. So, before we start making excuses, let's consider the point James made: no *man* can tame the tongue, but the Holy Spirit can.

The same Holy Spirit who activated God's words at creation, who blew life into our souls, who raised Jesus from the dead, who empowered the early church, who breathed upon the Scriptures, and who cleansed our hearts from sin is the same Spirit who can become a "bit" in our mouths. A bridled tongue is a mark of spiritual maturity (see James 3:2). It indicates that we've surrendered our entire lives to the lordship of Christ—mind, body, and spirit. Our impulse to have the last word, say what we think, or return insult for insult are all governed by the Holy Spirit.

Every word Jesus spoke was Spirit-sourced (John 6:63 and 12:49), and we can become just like Him (Luke 6:40). Our tongues can become a source of grace and edification (Ephesians 4:29; Colossians 4:6). We can learn to speak the truth in love (Ephesians 4:15). With the guidance of Holy Spirit, we can even release life-giving words that can alter the eternal trajectory of someone's life.

May we always be sourced with Holy Spirit and, like Jesus, speak words of Spirit and life.

QUESTIONS

1. Have you been around someone with an unbridled tongue? If so, what was your experience?

2. Do you speak with an unbridled tongue? Why or why not?

3. What are some ways that you can mature spiritually and speak with a bridled tongue?

If you choose to extend this lesson for one week, then complete the following questions and applications each day.

DAY 2   QUESTIONS
& Applications

1. Read James 1:26. What are your observations?

2. Read James 3:2. What are your observations?

3. Prayer for today: *Lord, may your Spirit bridle my tongue.*

DAY 3 — QUESTIONS & Applications

1. Read James 3:8. What do you think James meant when he said no one can tame the tongue?

2. Referring to James 3:8, what are poisonous words? Have you ever spoken with poisonous words? How can you prevent speaking with poisonous words?

3. Prayer for today: *Lord, free me from speaking poisonous words.*

DAY 4 — QUESTIONS & Applications

1. Read James 4:1–2. Where do you see an example of an unbridled tongue in these verses?

2. Describe how you would handle relational conflict with a bridled tongue?

3. How can you feel the emotion of anger but not speak with an unbridled tongue?

4. Prayer for today: *Lord, empower me to speak gracefully to others.*

DAY 5 QUESTIONS
& Applications

1. Read James 4:11–12. How do these verses relate to an unbridled tongue? What does it mean to speak *against* someone?

2. Read James 4:13–17. What are your observations? How do these verses relate to an unbridled tongue?

3. Reflecting on James 4:17, is speaking with an unbridled tongue sin?

4. Prayer for today: *Lord, empower me to not speak against someone.*

DAY 6 QUESTIONS
& Applications

1. Read James 5:7–9. What are your observations from these verses?

2. Reflecting on this passage, does impatience effect your words? If so, why?

3. Reflecting on James 5:9, do you complain against others? Why or why not?

4. Prayer for today: *Lord, today I will live in rest with you.*

DAY 7 QUESTIONS
& Applications

1. Read Ephesians 4:29. Is there an example of speaking with an unbridled tongue in this verse? What would a bridled tongue look like from this verse?

2. Reflecting on this week, have you spoken with a bridled tongue? Why or why not?

3. Describe what your life would look like if you consistently spoke with a bridled tongue with coworkers, friends, and family members.

4. Prayer for today: *Lord, my life will be shaped with a Spirit-empowered tongue.*

LESSON 12

An Argumentative Spirit

My college degree was in communications, and a specific course I was required to take was called "Persuasion: The Art of Arguing." Just imagine spending an entire semester learning how to defend and argue your point, whether it was correct or not, and how to persuade other people to agree. It created some interesting conversations with my wife, who, by the way, won almost every debate we had, and she never took the course.

There is an innate tendency in human beings to argue. Arguing differs greatly from expressing your ideas or opinions. Great decisions can be made through healthy discussion. Moreover, environments that encourage honest and transparent dialogue tend to thrive as opposed to repressed, dictatorial organizations. When people have the freedom to voice their opinions, even contrary views, it can help organizations reevaluate what is most essential, avoid pitfalls, loss of vision, and ineffectiveness. However, an argumentative spirit is something altogether different.

The Bible warns against arguing. Proverbs 17:14 (NLT) says, "Starting a quarrel is like opening a floodgate, so stop before a dispute breaks out." Paul wrote in Philippians 2:14, "Do all things without . . . disputing." And he said in Titus 3:9, "Avoid foolish controversies . . . ." Arguing, disputing, and controversies are rooted in division, a divisive spirit. The spirit behind the debate is an unwillingness to bend or find common ground. A person who is argumentative will become contentious, combative, and quarrelsome, and they are unwilling to see the damage they cause by defending their thoughts, ideas, or opinions.

Paul was addressing leaders when he wrote, "It is a trustworthy statement: if any man aspires to the office of overseer, it is a fine work he desires *to do*. An overseer, then, must be above reproach, the husband of one wife, temperate, prudent, respectable, hospitable, able to teach, not addicted to wine or pugnacious" (1 Timothy 3:1–3a). Note the word pugnacious; it's used only one other time in Titus 1:7.

Pugnacious (*plektes*) describes someone quick to debate, someone who is ready for a blow or poised for combat. It stems from a root word that means to flatten out by pounding, inflict with calamity, or to smite someone. Paul was stating that if people thought they were mature enough to be leaders but couldn't resist destroying people because they liked to argue, they have been deceived concerning the nature of their hearts. People who are pugnacious don't consider the result of their arguing, and they will defend their point of view regardless the cost to others, groups, or organizations.

In 2 Timothy 2:14, Paul warned against wrangling (*logomacheo*), which is another word used for arguing. This compound word, used only once in the New Testament, is so detrimental that Paul said that it will lead to "the ruin of the hearers." Paul continued a few verses later, "But avoid worldly *and* empty chatter, for it will lead to further ungodliness, and their talk will spread like gangrene" (2 Timothy 2:16–17a).

Can you see the demise of an argumentative spirit? It doesn't infect just one person, but it spreads throughout an organization. Innocent bystanders get sucked into the vortex of empty, barren words. Debates over who is right and who is wrong add tension to relationships and consumes valuable time. Soon, lines are drawn, sides are established, and the growth and health of the organization dies.

We might expect that scenario in a business or company that doesn't place a high value on Christian values, but Paul was addressing believers with the problem of arguing. Just imagine, for a moment, the ramifications of an argumentative and pugnacious believer in a local church. Perhaps this argumentative spirit contributes to the establishment of so many churches in one city or new churches starting in specific area.

Paul concluded, "The Lord's bond-servant must not be quarrelsome, but be kind to all, able to teach, patient when wronged" (2 Timothy 2:24). Quarrelsome is taken from a word that means armed for war. It describes someone who is quick to defend, strive, or argue. Paul advised, however, that the Lord's servant should be kind, teachable, and patient with others, even when wronged. Considering that believers should be quick to listen and slow to speak (James 1:19), perhaps we don't need to have the last word, even if we're right. It is better to be righteous than it is to be right. It's a tragedy to win an argument but lose the relationship.

Why do believers argue and quarrel? If it causes untold destruction in relationships, why do it? After thirty years of pastoring, I saw my share of arguing in the church. Board meetings and staff meetings sometimes became animated with raised voices, red faces, and veins popping as people argued their causes. Certainly, there are times when a cause needs to be defended, and as a pastor I can remember building strong cases for agendas that I believed needed to be supported.

But a pugnacious, argumentative spirit is different. According to James, conflicts, quarrels, and contentions are sourced in selfishness (James 4:1). James is describing someone who is so bent on his own viewpoint that he won't consider seeing someone else's perspective. Basically, they are right and everyone else is wrong. They are often persuasive and manipulative to the point of giving ultimatums. In the end, they will defend their causes even to the peril of relationships.

In the wake of an argumentative person, we find fallen comrades. These are people who once shared community with this individual, but they didn't have the courage or ability to withstand their unyielding spirits. But a pugnacious person doesn't really care who gets lost along the way if those remaining agree with him. This is the epitome of a self-sourced person.

Paul wrote, "Therefore, if anyone cleanses himself from these *things*, he will be a vessel for honor, sanctified, useful to the Master, prepared for every good work" (2 Timothy 2:21). In the context, "these things" that we are to cleanse ourselves from are arguing, wrangling, quarreling, and empty chatter. Our effectiveness to do good work for our Master will remain impaired if those activities are a part of our lives.

Let's choose to become sanctified vessels for the Lord's use. Let's cease being argumentative people.

QUESTIONS

1. Are you a contentious, argumentative person? (Look at the last ten years of your life.) If you are, what would you be willing to do to stop?

2. How can you become gentler with people—especially those who oppose you?

3. Are you prepared to be used by God for every good work? Why or why not?

If you choose to extend this lesson for one week, then complete
the following questions and applications each day.

DAY 2 QUESTIONS
& Applications

1. Read 2 Timothy 2:14–16. What are your observations?

2. Verse 16 (NASB) tells us to avoid worldly and empty
   chatter. What does that mean? How does this lead to
   ungodliness?

3. Prayer for today: *Lord, keep my mouth free of empty chatter.*

DAY 3 QUESTIONS
& Applications

1. Read 2 Timothy 2:23–26. What are your observations?

2. According to verse 24, what is our response instead of
   arguing and quarreling?

3. According to verse 25, how should you handle opposition?
   Does this describe you? Why or why not?

4. Prayer for today: *Lord, enable me to become a doer
   of your word.*

DAY 4 — QUESTIONS & Applications

1. Read Titus 3:9. What are your observations? Have you ever engaged in a foolish argument? If so, why?

2. Read Philippians 2:14–15. What are your observations?

3. Prayer for today: *Lord, I will do all things without arguing.*

DAY 5 — QUESTIONS & Applications

1. Read James 4:1–4. What are your observations? According to James, what are reasons for quarreling and conflicts?

2. According to verse 2, how does envy create arguments? How does that affect prayer?

3. Is it possible to be a friend of God and have wrong motives? Why or why not?

4. Prayer for today: *Lord, source me with your Spirit.*

DAY 6   QUESTIONS
& Applications

1. Read Proverbs 15:1 and 17:14, 27. What direction do these verses give to avoid arguments?

2. Do these verses describe your life? Why or why not?

3. Do you know someone who never argues (who is gentle and patient)? If so, describe the characteristics of their life.

4. Prayer for today: *Lord, I will be gentle and patient.*

DAY 7   QUESTIONS
& Applications

1. Reflecting on this week, did you avoid arguing with anyone? If not, why?

2. Would people describe you as being argumentative? If so, why?

3. What practical steps can you take to live without arguing or disputing? Write these steps down and review them often.

4. Prayer for today: *Lord, thank you for freeing me from an argumentative spirit.*

LESSON 13

A Righteous Mouth

Righteousness is a word that is woven through the entire Bible. In Hebrew righteousness, (*tsadaq*), has a two-fold meaning: to be declared right before God and mankind. It implies that a person has received deliverance from condemnation and, therefore, is viewed by God as morally clean. Some scholars describe being righteous as having a correct relationship upward and outward. If our relationship with God is right (upward), then our relationship with people will be right (outward). That description, then, would demonstrate righteousness.

The Greek (*dikaios*) word for righteous expands in the New Testament. We're not merely declared righteous, but through Christ we *become* righteous. For example, Paul wrote, "For if by the transgression of the one, death reigned through the one, much more those who receive the abundance of grace and of the gift of righteousness will reign in life through the One, Jesus Christ" (Romans 5:17). Being righteous is more than a declaration, it becomes an impartation. We receive the "gift of righteousness" that empowers us to live right before God and mankind.

Another example is 2 Corinthians 5:21, "He made Him who knew no sin *to be* sin on our behalf, so that we might become the righteousness of God in Him." Christ became what we were, which is sin, so that we could become what He is, righteousness. The verb "become" means that through Christ we have a new existence; we exist as the righteousness of God. Because we become the righteousness of God, our lives are transformed from the inside out. His righteousness is in us, enabling us to replicate the nature and life of Christ.

What does this have to do with the words that we speak? Everything. The Bible addresses the path of the righteous (Proverbs 4:18), the memory of the righteous (Proverbs 10:7), the wages of the righteous (Proverbs 10:16), the root of the righteous (Proverbs 12:3), the thoughts of the righteous (Proverbs 12:5), the house of the righteous (Proverbs 12:7), the way of the righteous (Proverbs 12:28), the light of the righteous (Proverbs 13:9), and the prayer of the righteous (Proverbs 15:29). So, it shouldn't surprise us that the Word addresses the mouth of the righteous (Proverbs 10:11).

Just imagine standing before God and being found without sin, even in the words we speak. That hope can only be accomplished by the gift of righteousness. God's righteousness permeates and recreates every aspect of our lives, and that includes the use of our tongues. With the New Testament understanding of righteous, let's examine the mouth of the righteous through the lens of Proverbs 10. In this chapter, there are five benefits of having a righteous mouth.

First, a righteous mouth is a fountain of life (verse 11). A fountain describes a constant flow of fresh water, unlike a pool stagnate body of water. A righteous person becomes a steady flow of words that imparts life to others. Every word Jesus spoke was filled with life (John 6:63). His words pierced the darkness and, therefore, raised the dead, empowered the lame, and liberated the demon possessed. Jesus' words were a fountain of life. The mouth and spoken words of the righteous becomes a reflection of the nature and character of Christ.

Second, a righteous mouth is like choice silver (verse 20). A common practice in the Old Testament was to purify silver by heating it to a specific temperature. At the desired temperature, dross or impurities would float and were skimmed off the top. Silver was considered pure when someone could see his reflection in it. Malachi wrote, "He will sit as a smelter and purifier of silver, and He will purify the sons of Levi and refine them like gold and silver, so that they may present to the Lord offerings in righteousness" (Malachi 3:3).

When God purifies us, the words we offer are like refined silver. There is value to our words because they are not filled with dross. A righteous tongue has been cleansed. As a child, my mother liberally applied a bar of soap to my mouth because my mouth and words reflected the dross I heard on the playground. She did a bit of refining so that my words wouldn't reflect the world. The mouth of the righteous releases refined words filled with heavenly content.

Third, a righteous mouth is a source of food (verse 21). Jesus said we would be held accountable for every careless word that we spoke (Matthew 12:36). Careless is derived from a word that means barren or lifeless. Careless words offer no value, hope, or life to hearers. In fact, those words can be harmful to listeners. A righteous mouth, however, releases words packed with nutrition. People are strengthened and exhorted when they hear a righteous person speak.

Fourth, a righteous mouth flows with wisdom (verse 31). Wisdom is the primary focus of the book of Proverbs. Wisdom is divine reasoning, and it equips us to reign over the issues in life that can cause so many to stumble. Through wisdom, we learn to manage family, friends, money, difficulties, future decisions, and, in fact, all of life. Wisdom is supreme, better than rubies and worth more than gold and silver (Proverbs 8:11 and 16:16).

James said, "But the wisdom from above is first pure, then peaceable, gentle, reasonable, full of mercy and good fruits, un-wavering, without hypocrisy" (James 3:17). These characteristics describe the mouth of the righteous. When a righteous person speaks, they release heavenly solutions to earthly problems. I remember spending an afternoon with someone whose life is filled with righteousness. I listened intently and told them that listening to them was like having a chiropractor adjust me on the inside. Their words aligned me to the realities of heaven.

Fifth, a righteous mouth brings forth what is acceptable (verse 32). A clearer translation would be a righteous mouth speaks words that are fitting, helpful, and favorable for the moment. These are not flattering words aimed at making a person merely feel better on an emotional level. The word acceptable in this verse means a righteous person gushes with timely words that fill a need. Put a wounded, needy person in front of a righteous person, and his heart will be ministered to by the life-giving words released.

Make today the start of consistently speaking with a righteous mouth.

QUESTIONS

1. Are you walking in righteousness with God? If not, why? If you are, describe what righteousness looks like in your life.

2. Reflecting on Proverbs 10, are those five characteristics flowing from your mouth? Why or why not?

3. What are some ways you have found to sustain a righteous life?

> If you choose to extend this lesson for one week, then complete the following questions and applications each day.

DAY 2 — QUESTIONS & Applications

1. Look up these nine characteristics of righteousness:

2. Proverbs 4:18, 10:7, 16; 12:3, 5, 7, 28; 13:9; 15:29

3. How do these passages speak to you? Have you found other characteristics of righteousness in Proverbs? If so, where?

4. Prayer for today: *Lord, thank you for your gift of righteousness.*

DAY 3 — QUESTIONS & Applications

1. Read Proverbs 10:11. In what ways is life released through your mouth?

2. Is life given to others through the words you speak? If not, why?

3. According to Proverbs 10:11, what is the opposite of a righteous mouth?

4. Prayer for today: *Lord, let the words of my mouth be filled with life.*

DAY 4 — QUESTIONS & Applications

1. Read Proverbs 10:31. In what practical ways can wisdom be imparted to others through you? Is wisdom found in your words? If so, how?

2. According to Proverbs 10:31, what is a perverted tongue? What are the consequences of speaking with that kind of tongue?

3. Prayer for today: *Lord, fill my mouth with wisdom.*

DAY 5 — QUESTIONS & Applications

1. Read Philippians 1:11. Describe what the fruit of righteousness looks like. What characteristics in your life demonstrate fruit of righteousness?

2. Do you know people who have fruit of righteousness? Describe their characteristics.

3. Prayer for today: *Lord, today I will bear righteous fruit.*

DAY 6 QUESTIONS
& Applications

1. Read 2 Corinthians 5:21. What are your observations?

2. Read 2 Corinthians 5:14–20. What characteristics in these verses demonstrate righteousness? In what ways would this passage effect the words you say?

3. Prayer for today: *Lord, thank you that I am the righteousness of God.*

DAY 7 QUESTIONS
& Applications

1. Reflecting on this week, how was righteousness demonstrated in your life? How did righteousness alter the words you chose to use this week?

2. What steps will you take to live with a mouth of righteousness?

3. Prayer for today: *Lord, my mouth will demonstrate the righteousness of God.*

LESSON 14

Wise and Foolish Words

No one can read the book of Proverbs without realizing the central emphasis on wisdom. In chapter one, Solomon wrote, "Wisdom shouts in the street, she lifts her voice in the square; at the head of the noisy *streets* she cries out; at the entrance of the gates in the city she utters her sayings: 'How long, O naive ones, will you love being simple-minded? And scoffers delight themselves in scoffing and fools hate knowledge? Turn to my reproof, behold, I will pour out my spirit on you; I will make my words known to you'" (Proverbs 1:20–23).

We are told to "make our ear attentive to wisdom" (Proverbs 2:2a) and we'll be blessed when we find it (Proverbs 3:13a). Why? "For her profit is better than the profit of silver and her gain better than fine gold. She is more precious than jewels; and nothing you desire compares with her. Long life is in her right hand; in her left hand are riches and honor. Her ways are pleasant ways, and all her paths are peace. She is a tree of life to those who take hold of her, and happy are all who hold her fast" (Proverbs 3:14–18).

In both the Old and New Testaments, wisdom essentially refers to spiritual revelation, which is functioning with divine reasoning. As I said in the last lesson, wisdom enables us to offer heavenly solutions to earthly problems. One scholar said wisdom is a Spirit-sourced mind, meaning that we consistently perceive life from a kingdom perspective.

James contrasted earthly wisdom with heavenly wisdom. He stated that earthly wisdom is sensual and demonic in nature. This *wisdom* is rooted in selfish ambition and, therefore, gives rise to disorder and every evil practice (James 3:15–16). Just imagine the kind of words spoken from the mouth of someone sourced with earthly wisdom.

This would mean giving someone our fleshly words instead of God's words. Earthly sourced words would be an echo of the culture or the condition of our hearts, not a voice from heaven. A person sourced with earthly wisdom would share the latest gossip or social buzz instead of Spirit-led insight. Their words would be motivated by the flesh; therefore, they would likely encourage someone who is being insulted to fight back or retaliate. Their words would incite dissension not unity because the Spirit of God is not operative in their earthly wisdom.

Years ago, while pastoring, I received a call from someone in my church who was upset with me and our leadership. They were very accusative in their words. They believed we were taking advantage of other people by doing a special fundraising dinner. Their understanding and view for the purpose of the dinner and the dissension they caused as they left the fellowship saddened me greatly. I later discovered that they were acting on the "wisdom" and advice of another Christian friend.

Earthly sourced wisdom is destructive. A person releasing words from this mindset will create an environment conducive for the enemy to operate. Wherever you observe evil and hurtful practices in people, they are acting in agreement with wisdom not sourced from the heavenlies.

In Proverbs, a person who rejects heavenly wisdom is compared to a fool. A fool will spurn reproof, correction, and insight that come from wisdom. Consequently, the writer says, "So they shall eat of the fruit of their own way and be satiated with their own devices. For the waywardness of the naive will kill them, and the complacency of fools will destroy them" (Proverbs 1:31–32). This sounds like someone sourced with earthly wisdom.

Words from the mouth of a foolish person will bring ruination to all who hear them (Proverbs 10:14). Their mouth will spout forth folly, a word that means someone lacking moral restraint (Proverbs 15:2). And, as already pointed out, a fool's lips will produce strife, disputes, and controversy (Proverbs 18:6). Therefore, the Bible says the beginning of wisdom—heavenly wisdom—is to get more wisdom (Proverbs 4:7). We will never speak right if we're not thinking right, and we won't think right without heavenly wisdom.

In contrast to earthly wisdom, James said, "But the wisdom from above is first of all pure (undefiled); then it is peace-loving, courteous (considerate, gentle). [*It is willing to*] yield to reason, full of compassion and good fruits; it is wholehearted *and* straightforward, impartial *and* unfeigned (free from doubts, wavering, and insincerity)" (James 3:17 Amplified Version).

Picture yourself having a conversation with someone sourced with heavenly wisdom. What kind of words do you believe you would hear, and do you think those words would touch to your heart?

According to James, wise words will be pure, peaceable, courteous, considerate, and gentle for starters. You will hear words from someone full of compassion and bearing good fruits. You probably would leave the conversation full of faith because you heard from someone without hypocrisy. According to Proverbs, wise words will be used sparingly (Proverbs 10:19), bring healing (Proverbs 12:18), and promote knowledge (Proverbs 15:7). The fact is wise words are filled with inspiration, hope, and revelation. It's like having heaven breathe on us.

Wisdom will give us discernment when to speak, where to speak, what to speak, and to whom to speak. It will teach us how to say what needs to be spoken, and it will teach us why we shouldn't utter what we are self-motivated to say. Wisdom will enable us to navigate through messy conflicts without amplifying them. If wisdom has dominated our conversation, there will be fewer opportunities for people to leave hurt, confused, and misunderstood.

There is only one place wisdom is attained. Proverbs says, "For the Lord gives wisdom; from His mouth come knowledge and understanding" (Proverbs 2:6). Proverbs 1:5 says, "A wise man will hear and increase in learning, and a man of understanding will acquire wise counsel." Let me suggest three things. First, a wise man will listen. This implies intimacy with the Lord. We must spend time with God and in His word if we hope to gain wisdom. Be careful of distractions and busyness because they are the detractors from His voice and will decrease our growth in wisdom.

Second, a wise man will increase learning. This means we must always remain teachable. No one is too wise to stop learning. A teachable person is likely to become a wise person. Third, a wise man will acquire godly counsel. This means we value discipleship, and we value hearing godly counsel from those with Spirit-sourced minds.

It's time to wise up.

QUESTIONS

1. Are you allowing wisdom to guide the words that you speak? Why or why not?

2. What are some ways you've found to increase wisdom in your life?

3. Can you identify three people you know who have wisdom? What are the characteristics of their lives?

If you choose to extend this lesson for one week, then complete
the following questions and applications each day.

DAY 2   QUESTIONS
& Applications

1. Read Proverbs 1:20–33. What are your observations?

2. What are some consequences of spurning wisdom and knowledge? According to verse 33, what happens when you turn to wisdom?

3. Prayer for today: *Lord, guard my heart from becoming foolish.*

DAY 3   QUESTIONS
& Applications

1. Read Proverbs 2:1–5. What are your observations?

2. According to verse 5, what are the blessings of wisdom?

3. Prayer for today: *Lord, give me discernment today.*

DAY 4 QUESTIONS
& Applications

1. Read Proverbs 2:6–22. What are your observations?

2. Verse 11 (NASB) says, "Discretion will guard you." In what ways are you guarded according to verses 12–16?

3. Prayer for today: *Lord, may discretion keep me from evil.*

DAY 5 QUESTIONS
& Applications

1. Read Proverbs 24:1–7. What are your observations?

2. Verse 7 (NIV) says, "Wisdom is too high for fools; in the assembly at the gate they must not open their mouths." What does it mean that wisdom is too high for a fool? What does it mean that a fool has nothing to say?

3. Prayer for today: *Lord, may my words be filled with wisdom.*

DAY 6   QUESTIONS
& Applications

1. Read James 3:13–18. In what ways is heavenly wisdom contrasted with earthly wisdom?

2. According to this passage, what kind of words would you speak if sourced by heavenly wisdom?

3. Prayer for today: *Lord, source me with heavenly wisdom.*

DAY 7   QUESTIONS
& Applications

1. Reflecting on this week, were you sourced with heavenly wisdom or earthly wisdom? How did you demonstrate what you were sourced with?

2. Describe words you spoke in wisdom this last week?

3. What is your plan to live each day sourced with heavenly wisdom? (See Proverbs 1:5.)

4. Prayer for today: *Lord, may my words and actions reflect heavenly wisdom.*

LESSON 15

Imparting Grace

In the New Testament, the Greek word for grace is *charis*. It's an interesting word with a variety of meanings, but historically, it is derived from a secular term that referred to superhuman abilities. In Greek literature, if you were favored by the gods, then you were granted *charis* (grace) that resulted in supernatural manifestations. In other words, someone couldn't be given grace without it enabling them to do something extraordinary. Therefore, in the Greek mindset, grace equaled transforming power.

In the Old Testament, Zerubbabel was given the responsibility of rebuilding the temple that had been torn down by the Babylonians when Israel was taken into captivity. All that remained of the temple was a mountain of rubble, stone, and rocks, and Judah's enemies were attempting to foil every rebuilding endeavor. But Zerubbabel was given a word from the Lord to shout grace before the insurmountable mess that lay before him (Zechariah 4:7). Grace? Yes, grace carried the power to remove stones, eliminate problems, destroy fear, and route enemies.

With that backdrop in mind, we learn that grace is much more than a bestowment of God's unmerited favor—which is the standard definition. Grace is a bestowment of power. It's a divine force granted to believers that empowers them with supernatural gifts (see 1 Corinthians 12:8–10). Grace will produce an inward change that is always manifested with outward evidence. You cannot be given grace and no one know it. It's not a stealth bestowment; there will always be fruit and evidence that you have been touched by grace.

Think about the implications of being saved by grace (Ephesians 2:8). Can one truly be rescued, redeemed, and delivered by grace and no one know? Of course not, Paul continued to write that once we've been saved by grace, "We are His workmanship, created in Christ Jesus for good works" (Ephesians 2:10a). Grace will be expressed through good works. An encounter with grace not only effects your life, but it also ripples into the lives you touch.

Think about how grace might affect the words you speak. Paul wrote, "Let no unwholesome word proceed from your mouth, but only such *a word* as is good for edification according to the need *of the moment,* so that it will give grace to those who hear" (Ephesians 4:29). Note the phrase about giving grace to those who hear. You have a scriptural commission to impart grace to your hearers. Without grace, your words might reflect bitterness, anger, clamor, slander, and unforgiveness (Ephesians 4:31–32).

Instead, grace-filled words can impart power, freedom, and strength. Like Zerubbabel, you can empower people to overcome insurmountable obstacles that stand before them by speaking grace into their lives. Your words can bring deliverance from fear, anxiety, and oppression. According to Romans 5:20, grace is strong enough to extend beyond the effects of sin, which means your words have the capacity to deliver people from the tyranny of sin and its consequences.

Continuing with Ephesians 4:29, Paul said the words that come from our mouths should *only* be good for edification. This little word only (*ei*) is called a conditional conjunction meaning that grace has not been adequately imparted if we haven't spoken edifying words. To explain this differently, grace-filled words will always edify; edification is the result of releasing grace into people's lives.

Edification (*oikodome*) describes building a house in such a manner that it will remain stable through adversity, such as a raging storm. It's not only structurally strong but well-protected by a substantial roof. To edify people is to build up (not puff up) their lives with encouraging words, enabling them to remain steadfast against challenging circumstances, and speaking truthful words that keep their minds protected against the enemy's schemes.

There was a season in my life when adversity assailed me on every side. During that time, my friend, Pastor Corey Jones, spoke words to me that were full of grace. I felt an impartation of healing wash over my life, and I was empowered to prevail through the difficulties my family and I were walking through. Words of grace are meant to heal not hurt. They are truthful words spoken in love, and listeners will become spiritually stronger and healthier because of hearing them.

In Colossians 4:6, Paul wrote, "Let your speech always be with grace, *as though* seasoned with salt, so that you will know how you should respond to each person." The adverb always (*pantote*) simply means at all times, on every occasion. We are to speak with grace to others every time we open our mouths, regardless of what they are saying or doing to us. This idea is underscored by using salt as a metaphor. Much like a preservative, grace-filled words preserve so what we say is consistently edifying in all circumstances.

As we travel the country for ministry, we are often faced with circumstances where we have a choice concerning how we choose to release our words. I'm reminded of one such opportunity where we had driven several hundred miles and were hoping to pull our coach in, hook up, get changed, and begin the service. What we discovered, however, was that the needed access for water, electricity, or sewage had not been prepared for quick access, as promised. This was my moment to release grace-filled words, even in my exhortation of how to correct the situation.

Words that impart grace still speak truth; they still challenge, encourage, and inspire people to be better than they are. Parents can speak with grace when correcting children. Pastors can speak with grace when confronting sin. Leaders and CEO's can speak with grace when managing businesses. Grace should fill our speech no matter who we are, where we are, what we do, or who we are speaking to. Our words should never be empty and hollow but edifying, healing, and life-giving.

Graceful words are empowered by the Spirit of God, not people or circumstances. When we learn to speak grace over everything around us, we'll start to experience the power contained within grace. Grace is an impartation of a kingdom reality over an earthly issue. Speaking grace is a practical way of fulfilling the mandate of bringing heaven to earth (see Matthew 6:10).

Let's impart grace with our words.

QUESTIONS

1. How would you define grace?

2. Have you experienced the power of grace-filled words in your life? If so, explain.

3. What can you do to speak words of grace *only* and *always*?

> If you choose to extend this lesson for one week, then complete
> the following questions and applications each day.

DAY 2 — QUESTIONS & Applications

1. Zechariah 4:7 (Amplified) says, "What are you,
   O great mountain [of obstacles]? Before Zerubbabel
   [who will rebuild the temple] *you will become* a plain
   (insignificant)! And he will bring out the capstone
   [of the new temple] with loud shouts of "Grace, grace
   to it!" Why do you believe the Lord instructed
   Zerubbabel to shout grace at the mountain?

2. What are some obstacles in your life that require grace
   to deal with?

3. Prayer for today: *Lord, empower me to speak grace over
   my challenges.*

DAY 3 — QUESTIONS & Applications

1. Read Romans 5:20–21. How is the power of grace demonstrated in these verses? How does grace abound over sin?

2. Read Romans 6:1–2. What are your observations?

3. How do you think these two passages would shape the way
   you speak to others?

4. Prayer for today: *Lord, transform my life through grace.*

DAY 4 — QUESTIONS & Applications

1. Read Ephesians 4:29–30. Do you believe speaking non-graceful words can grieve the Holy Spirit? If so, how?

2. In reference to Ephesians 4:29, how do you practically give grace to those who hear?

3. Describe what a day speaking grace might look like for you. What circumstances will be most challenging?

4. Prayer for today: *Lord, today I will speak grace to those who hear.*

DAY 5 — QUESTIONS & Applications

1. Read Colossians 4:6. What are your observations? What does it mean to have speech seasoned with salt?

2. Read Colossians 4:5. Describe the connection between verses 5 and 6.

3. Prayer for today: *Lord, I will influence others toward Christ with my words.*

DAY 6 — QUESTIONS & Applications

1. Read 1 Peter 3:8–9. What are your observations?

2. In the above passage, how are graceful words demonstrated?

3. Prayer for today: *Lord, empower me to bless those who may insult me.*

DAY 7 — QUESTIONS & Applications

1. Describe how God's grace has transformed your life.

2. Reflecting on this week, describe how you imparted grace to others with your words.

3. How can you become known as a person full of grace? (See Acts 6:8.)

4. Prayer for today: *Lord, I will be known as someone full of grace.*

LESSON 16

Speaking Prophetic Words

I once made the comment that we either speak prophetic words or pathetic words. Usually, the difference is in the source of our words. First Corinthians 14:1 says, "Pursue love, yet earnestly desire spiritual *gifts*, but especially that you may prophesy." There are two commands in this verse that expand our understanding concerning speaking prophetic words.

The first command is to pursue love. The word pursue (*doiko*) is a present imperative. A present tense verb indicates that the action doesn't stop. We could translate this word as pursing, chasing, or seeking. One expositor said this word could be translated as hunting. Because it is an imperative in Greek, it makes the action a command. So, we're commanded to never stop pursing, chasing, or seeking love; we're to pursue love like a hunter does its prey.

Our ministry's name is, *Becoming Love Ministries*. Our team believes we're never to stop growing in our capacity to become love. The second command in this verse is to earnestly desire. These two words are derived from the Greek word *zeloo*. This word is also a present imperative, which is a command to keep desiring or craving something with great affection.

What are we to continually desire? The answer is not gifts because that word is italicized in most translations, which means it's not in the actual text. Instead, we are to keep desiring spiritual (*pneumatikos*), a compound word that means one who is perpetually governed and sourced by the Holy Spirit. Therefore, this is a command to constantly desire being influenced, governed, and sourced by the Holy Spirit every moment of our lives.

This verse, however, is very specific in the manner we are to be perpetually sourced. Note, "especially that you may prophesy." To prophesy simply means to say what you hear the Spirit saying to you. Sometimes He will prompt us to speak a very specific word to someone we may not know. In that moment, we are simply the instrument that God wants His words to be spoken through. In other words, He sources us with words to speak, and they become prophetic words—Spirit-sourced words for someone.

A few years ago, I finished a service on a Sunday morning, and as I was leaving the church to travel to my next assignment, a man gave me $100. I thanked him and put the bill in my pocket. That evening, before the next series of services began, I was eating dinner with the pastor. As the meal progressed, it became obvious that the waitress was having a bad day. She was rude and impatient with us, the meal was incorrect, and the water glasses were empty. But I was pursuing love, so her behavior wasn't offensive to me, and I also wanted to avail my life to the Holy Spirit so that she would encounter Jesus. However, I was unprepared for what the Lord prompted me to do next.

God spoke clearly and told me to give her the $100. In my spirit, I suggested to the Lord that I give her the $20 I had in my wallet, but that wasn't His word to me. I quickly relented and called her over to the table. I placed the money in her hand, smiled, and told her to be blessed. Instantly, she started to cry. I stood and hugged her, and the atmosphere of the restaurant shifted. I believe love is the atmosphere of heaven being manifested on earth.

In that very moment, the Spirit sourced me with words to speak to her. They were precise words aimed directly at her heart, and they ministered profoundly to her. When we consistently pursue love and intentionally desire to be sourced by the Spirit, it's likely we're going to receive prophetic words for people. Don't be surprised when God speaks. As believers, we know the voice of our Shepherd (John 10:27). He will often give us words that minister to straying sheep around us.

The Bible says, "But one who prophesies speaks to men for edification and exhortation and consolation" (1 Corinthians 14:3). Prophetic words are not for you; they are words meant to encourage and benefit other people. We're simply the mouthpiece that God desires to use in the process. Jesus was perpetually sourced by the Spirit; consequently, His words were filled with life, hope, and encouragement (John 6:63 and 12:49).

The Samaritan woman was so deeply touched by Jesus' prophetic words that she announced to her city, "He told me all things that I have done" (John 4:39b). As a result, many more Samaritans came to Jesus and believed when they heard His words. Like Jesus, we can speak Spirit-sourced words to those around us and many can come to know and believe in Him. The challenge for us is to remain in a position conducive to hearing Him speak. Let me suggest a few perspectives concerning prophetic words.

First, comply to the two commands of 1 Corinthians 14:1. Never stop pursuing love and never stop desiring to be sourced by the Holy Spirit. The next time you go to Walmart, think about what it might look like to pursue love and be sourced by the Holy Spirit while in the store. With thoughts like these in your mind, you're better positioned and ready to be used by the Lord.

Second, believe that your life matters enough to the Lord that He desires to use you. I believe many Christians hear the Lord, but His words are sabotaged by our negative thoughts such as, "Why would God speak to me?" or "I'm not worthy to be used by God." You've been qualified by Christ. He has called you and given you a ministry of reconciliation (2 Corinthians 5:18). That means by calling, everywhere you go He wants to use you to bring God and people together (the meaning of reconciliation). He desires to speak to you and through you to minister to others.

Third, when you hear a word for someone else, don't over-analyze it. Remember, it's not for you. You are the messenger sent to deliver the word, not critique the message. A friend of mine was praying for someone and stopped and said, "For whatever reason, I hear the word buffalo; and I'm to tell you buffalo is the answer." The other person was considering a job in Buffalo, NY, and asked God for clear direction if this move was to occur. They are fulfilling God's call in New York because someone was used by God to speak prophetically.

Let's live our lives in such a way that we speak prophetic words—Spirit-sourced words to a world that needs to hear from the Lord.

QUESTIONS

1. Have you ever spoken a prophetic word to another person, or has someone speak one to you? If so, describe your experience.

2. What are some ways you can learn to hear the voice of the Lord in your life?

3. Do you love and value people the way Jesus does? If you do, describe what that looks like. If not, why?

If you choose to extend this lesson for one week, then complete the following questions and applications each day.

DAY 2
QUESTIONS
& Applications

1. Read 1 Corinthians 14:1. What are some practical ways you can keep pursuing love? How can you keep increasing your desire for the Holy Spirit's influence?

2. The word "spiritual" means being governed or sourced by the Holy Spirit. What does that look like in your life?

3. Prayer for today: *Lord, source me with your Spirit.*

DAY 3 QUESTIONS & Applications

1. In reference to 1 Corinthians 14:1, what does prophecy mean to you? Do you desire to speak prophetically? Why or why not?

2. Read 1 Corinthians 14:3. What are your observations? What are the benefits of speaking prophetically? Why are prophetic words such a great benefit to others?

3. Prayer for today: *Lord, speak through me so I can minister to others.*

DAY 4 QUESTIONS & Applications

1. Read 1 Corinthians 14:24–25. What are your observations? According to verse 25, what are the results of a church speaking prophetically?

2. In reference to 1 Corinthians 14:24–25, how is it possible for "all" to prophesy in the church? Have you ever witnessed that happening? If so, describe your experience. What does it mean to have the secrets of your heart exposed by prophetic words?

3. Prayer for today: *Lord, use me to bring people to you.*

DAY 5 — QUESTIONS & Applications

1. Read John 4:1–18. What are your observations?

2. In reference to John 4:1–18, how was Jesus pursing love in this conversation? How did Jesus speak prophetically to this woman? How were hidden things revealed?

3. Read John 4:39–41. What was the outcome to Jesus' words to the Samaritan woman?

4. Prayer for today: *Lord, use me to speak to spiritually lost people.*

DAY 6 — QUESTIONS & Applications

1. Read John 10:1–5 and 10:27. Do you hear Jesus' voice? How does He speak to you? Have you ever heard Him speak something to you for someone else?

2. Read Luke 10:38–42. What are your observations? How can you live *listening* to the words of the Lord?

3. Prayer for today: *Lord, help me to hear every word you speak.*

DAY 7   QUESTIONS
& Applications

1. Reflecting on this week, did you sense the Lord leading you to minister to anyone? Have you spoken prophetically over anyone? If so, describe that experience.

2. What are some practical ways to eliminate distractions from your life and to intensify a listening heart?

3. This coming week, before entering a store, restaurant, work, or church, ask the Lord to use you to minister to people you are around. Ask Him to give you prophetic words.

4. Prayer for today: *Lord, I am listening.*

LESSON 17

Words of Encouragement

Hebrews 3:13 says, "But encourage one another day after day, as long as it is *still* called 'Today,' so that none of you will be hardened by the deceitfulness of sin." This verse is sandwiched between two important truths. First, don't fall away from the Lord (verse 12). Second, hold firm until the end (verse 14). Both truths are held together by a single command we are to follow daily.

The writer instructs us to encourage (*parakaleo*) one another. This word has several meanings such as: to call someone to action, to invite someone to fulfill a task, to give comfort to someone, and to exhort someone. The definition that best fits the context is to strengthen someone with timely words. Our words are to inspire people, giving them the empowerment to remain steadfast in their faith.

Sin, on the other hand, is deceitful in its nature, and it entices people down a path toward unbelief. When unbelief overtakes the heart of a person, they cease being compliant to God's plans and desires for their lives. Eventually, they will "fall away

LIFE & DEATH: THE POWER OF WORDS

from the living God" (Hebrews 3:12b). The writer of Hebrews had in mind the faithless Israelites who fell prey to unbelief and their bodies were scattered in the wilderness (see Hebrews 3:16–19).

Against this backdrop, the writer instructs us to encourage each other. In fact, you'll note that "today" is the hour to do so, meaning don't delay; this assignment is too essential. Your encouraging words inspire people to action, they instill confidence and hope, and they empower people to remain faithful in their relationships with the Lord. A simple fact remains, people need encouragement. Truett Cathy, the founder of Chick-fil-A, said, "How do you know if a man needs encouragement? He is breathing." Live your life as an encourager and encourage everyone every single day.

Though raised in a Christian home, I strayed far from God until about age twenty. After my conversion, challenges buffeted me. I was a very poor student, reading on a fifth-grade level, and struggled to retain anything read. Relationships were few because I had damaged their ability to trust me, and so initially, I felt alone in my pursuit of God. About that time, I felt called to be a minister and to enroll in a Christian college. The summer before my enrollment, I felt prompted to share my conversion and call with an older pastor I knew all too well. We had a history of clashing, especially during summer camps when I was *always* in trouble. This pastor was the person who dealt the severest consequences.

Yet, my heart had truly changed. When I nervously told him what Christ was doing in my life, he didn't hesitate for a moment to speak words of encouragement into my young heart. That day he bought a book for me and wrote encouraging words in the cover. Then he looked at me and said, "Rob, you have the ability to be a great man of God."

What? Me? A great man of God? He gave me hope. His words were not spoken in flattery; they were given with genuineness and sincerity of heart. His encouragement strengthened my resolve to remain faithful to God's call, even though I struggled my first few years in college. To this day I desire to be a great man of God.

A few years later, it was a college professor who encouraged me to study and write about prayer. His encouragement spurred my meeting of Leonard Ravenhill, whose teachings and books have inspired people around the world. In graduate school, a professor positively critiqued an illustration I designed, and he later used it in one of his published works. On and on I could go, highlighting encouragement from others that has helped me to remain a partaker of Christ.

Let me be quick to point out that I don't look for encouragement from others. As believers, we have the abiding presence of the Holy Spirit who is called the Encourager. Ultimately, the Holy Spirit guides me, teaches me, comforts me, and shows me all things I need to know. Yet, from time to time, He will use another faithful follower to accomplish His purposes. That is a blessing found in Christian community. We pray for one another, teach one another, lift each other's burdens, and according to the writer of Hebrews, we encourage one another.

Learning to be an encourager starts with seeing people from God's perspective. The Bible says, "Therefore from now on we recognize no one according to the flesh" (2 Corinthians 5:16a). As believers, we don't see people for who they are; we see them for who they can be through the power and grace of God. We look upon others with spiritual eyes, not physical ones. We see people as victors over long-term sin, ugly habits, and crippling additions. Whatever they are in the flesh, God can transform their lives and character. Encouragement speaks to the potential of Christ's redeeming love.

We don't deny the reality of people's circumstances, but we refuse to allow their circumstances to influence what we believe. As followers of Christ, our perspectives have been altered, so our words of encouragement are rooted in the gospel. They are words filled with hope because our view of a particular situation is seen through the lens of what Christ can do. That's why people will often rise to the level of encouragement we have given them because our encouraging words are filled with the nature of Christ.

Encouragers are great listeners too. They won't dominate conversations; rather, they ask questions inviting people to share, which gives others an opportunity to talk about things of interest to them. I spent thirty minutes listening to a man talk about his paint collection. My questions and willingness to listen to him brought inspiration and life to his spirit for a few moments. As believers, we can create opportunities like this anywhere we go.

Speaking encouraging words is a daily assignment according to the writer of Hebrews. Day after day implies a lifestyle of giving encouragement no matter our circumstances. This gives purpose to each day. Take a brief inventory of whom you spend time with each day and then ask the Lord for encouraging words. Your words could avert disaster in someone. They could steer someone from the wrong path or keep them from making a regrettable decision. Most of all, your encouragement could help someone hold firm until the end (see Hebrews 3:14).

Just think, eternity might be filled with people you have encouraged.

QUESTIONS

1. How many people have you encouraged in the last seven days? Describe your experiences.

2. Who has been the biggest encourager in your life? What did they say or do to encourage you?

3. How can you live as an encourager to others?

If you choose to extend this lesson for one week, then complete the following questions and applications each day.

DAY 2 — QUESTIONS & Applications

1. Read Hebrews 3:12–14. What are your observations?

2. In this passage of Scripture, how does encouragement keep sin from hardening a person's heart?

3. Prayer for today: *Lord, may I help others have a tender heart.*

DAY 3 — QUESTIONS & Applications

1. Read Hebrews 10:23–25. What are your observations? What are practical ways to encourage people according to this passage?

2. What are your plans to activate these verses in your life? Explain.

3. Prayer for today: *Lord, make me an encourager.*

DAY 4 — QUESTIONS & Applications

1. Read 1 Thessalonians 5:9–11. What are your observations?

2. Read 1 Thessalonians 5:14. What are your observations? The NASB says, "Encourage the fainthearted." What does that mean?

3. Prayer for today: *Lord, I will encourage those discouraged.*

DAY 5 — QUESTIONS & Applications

1. A similar Greek word for encourage is used for the Holy Spirit (*parakletos*). It's generally translated as comforter, but the meaning is like the Greek word for encourage. Read John 14:16 and 26, 15:26, and 16:7. What are your observations?

2. In the context of these verses, how does the Holy Spirit comfort/encourage people?

3. Prayer for today: *Lord, you are my encourager.*

DAY 6 — QUESTIONS & Applications

1. The Holy Spirit as the comforter/encourager is also called, "the Spirit of truth." Read John 14:16–18 and 16:13. How are encouragement and truth related in these verses?

2. How has the Holy Spirit been a source of truth and encouragement to you in the last month? How can you be a source of truth and encouragement to others?

3. Prayer for today: *Lord, I will be a source of truth and encouragement.*

DAY 7 — QUESTIONS & Applications

1. Reflecting on this last week, what lessons have you learned about encouragement?

2. Who have you encouraged this week? Explain.

3. Who will you encounter in the next seven days? What are some practical ways you can encourage them?

4. Prayer for today: *Lord, thank you for the people I'm going to encourage.*

LESSON 18

The Power of Declaration

After spending nearly thirty years pastoring, we've heard our share of complaints from people walking through adverse situations. We all go through personal challenges, but we all don't prevail over those challenges. Instead, during adverse seasons many people start to speak forth their laments, such as, "This will never change," "I will never be free," "It goes from bad to worse," or, "We'll never see victory."

Statements like these have a negative effect on us when we release them from our mouths. As stated in an earlier lesson, words are not neutral. The Bible indicates that, "Death and life are in the power of the tongue" (Proverbs 18:21a). Caution should be taken when speaking lifeless words over ourselves.

The Bible says, "But My righteous one shall live by faith; and if he shrinks back, my soul has no pleasure in him" (Hebrews 10:38). We *live* by faith. That statement doesn't mean we merely survive; it means we prevail. Circumstances around us don't influence how we think or what we say because we're living by faith. According to the Bible, we are to look at unseen things, not things that can be seen (2 Corinthians

4:18). Things that are seen are temporal; they are here today but gone tomorrow. Things that are unseen belong to the kingdom realm, which makes them eternal.

Faith, then, looks beyond the earthly realm and focuses on the kingdom realm. We prevail by not becoming overwhelmed with earthly issues but by placing our attention on a superior reality. When we do so, we're enabled to live in victory regardless of what we walk through. Living by faith is usually evidenced by the words released from our mouths in times of difficulty.

In Hebrews 10:38, the writer indicated that God doesn't take pleasure in those who shrink back (*hupostello*). This verb has several meanings that are all tied to fear. One expositor said this verb describes someone who, because of fear, hesitates to avow what they believe. In other words, they don't speak words of faith. They have been overcome by the winds of adversity surrounding them, and they've lost sight of God's eternal perspective. People in this position often speak out of frustration, fear, and oppression.

This is illustrated in the Old Testament when the king of Aram wanted to capture Elisha. After learning that Elisha was in Dothan, he dispatched horses, chariots, and a great army to surround the entire city. Elisha's servant woke the next morning and was panic stricken by the sight of the circling army. He asked Elisha, "What shall we do?" (2 Kings 6:15b). His question is better translated, "How are we going to make it?" He was speaking from an earthly perspective, and as a result his words revealed fear and unbelief.

Elisha saw the situation from a kingdom viewpoint and realized a superior army stood with him. He was able to speak from faith and witness the power of God overcome the enemy. This story exemplifies for us the necessity to consistently look upon surrounding circumstances from heaven's vantage point. It is only then that we can declare with faith what God is able to do—no matter how threatening the situation looks.

We read in 2 Corinthians 4:13, "But having the same spirit of faith, according to what is written: 'I believed, therefore I spoke,' we also believe, therefore we also speak." Paul quoted Psalm 116:10 when the psalmist was experiencing affliction and persecution, yet amid his adversity he didn't shrink back. Regardless of circumstances, the psalmist spoke out of faith.

Faith doesn't deny the reality of difficult circumstances, but it doesn't allow those circumstances a place of influence in our lives. Because we're anchored by faith to a greater reality, we're able to speak from that posture. Our words, then, become a declaration of what God has done and what we believe He will do in future situations. Because we believe what has happened in us is greater than what might be happening to us, we won't shrink back, and we won't cease declaring our faith. What are you declaring over your life during times of uncertainty?

Cindy and I were challenged by this several years ago. We decided, despite circumstances, we wouldn't shrink back—we wouldn't cease declaring what we believed. So, we made a list of thirty-five faith statements and began declaring them over our lives regardless of the earthly circumstances. Rather than letting our words and prayers become filled with complaints, they became words rooted in faith. Every day our hearts were inspired with hope as we were reminded that His ways are greater than our circumstances.

Here is a list of eight of our declarations:

- We declare that we have the mind of Christ.

- We declare that we're seated in Christ far above the enemy.

- We declare that our mouths speak life and not death.

- We declare that Your Holy Spirit leads us into all truth.

- We declare that we're able to hear God's voice over every other voice.

- We declare that we're growing in a spirit of wisdom and revelation.

- We declare that we're free from being offended.

- We declare our lives are influencing others into a relationship with Christ.

These declarations are established on Scripture, so we speak His Word into our lives. Like Jesus taught us to pray, we declared His kingdom to come and manifest on earth like it was in heaven (Matthew 6:10). Amazingly, time and time again we saw the heavenly realm transform our earthly challenges.

I don't expect you to echo these same declarations. Ask the Holy Spirit what truth from His Word He wants you to

LIFE & DEATH: THE POWER OF WORDS

speak over your life and circumstances. Whatever you do, don't shrink back. Don't cease to avow your faith when you're surrounded by an army of despair. You cannot allow what you're going through to matter more than what should matter most. You are a child of the Lord God Most High, and He who is with you is greater than what stands against you.

QUESTIONS

1. Are you living by faith or shrinking back in fear? Describe how you know the difference?

2. Are words you release filled with faith? How would those closest to you answer that question?

3. Can you describe what your life might look like if you not only lived by faith, but your words were declarations of faith?

> If you choose to extend this lesson for one week, then complete
> the following questions and applications each day.

DAY 2 QUESTIONS
& Applications

1. Read Hebrews 10:35–39. What are your observations?

2. Why do you believe God has no pleasure in those
   who shrink back? Do you have some things in your
   life that tempt you to shrink back? If so, what
   are they?

3. Prayer for today: *Lord, empower me to never
   shrink back.*

DAY 3 QUESTIONS
& Applications

1. Read 2 Corinthians 4:16–18. What are your
   observations? How does a person practically live
   while looking at the unseen?

2. How would you define faith? How does faith effect
   the way you live?

3. Prayer for today: *Lord, I choose to look at the unseen.*

DAY 4 — QUESTIONS & Applications

1. Read 2 Kings 6:8–18. What are your observations?

2. Have you ever felt surrounded by challenging circumstances? If so, explain. How do you respond when the enemy attempts to surround you?

3. Prayer for today: *Lord, open my eyes to see your presence.*

DAY 5 — QUESTIONS & Applications

1. Read Psalm 27:1–6. What are your observations?

2. What was David's response when surrounded by the enemy? According to verse 6, what came forth from David's mouth?

3. What are some practical steps you can take to respond against pressure as David did?

4. Prayer for today: *Lord, I choose to speak words of praise no matter what.*

DAY 6 — QUESTIONS & Applications

1. King Jehoshaphat, the king of Judah, was being threaten by invading armies. Read what happened after Jehoshaphat consulted with the Lord (see 2 Chronicles 20:20–22). How do these verses minister to you?

2. What did the king commission his people to do? According to verse 21, what declaration did the people make aloud?

3. Prayer for today: *Lord, your lovingkindness is everlasting.*

DAY 7 — QUESTIONS & Applications

1. Reflecting on this week, what have you learned about declaring God's truths regardless of surrounding circumstances?

2. Make a list of eight declarations (feel free to rewrite the eight in this lesson) and proclaim them each day for the next four weeks. At the end of that period, evaluate the effectiveness. Ask the Lord if that practice should continue.

3. Prayer for today: *Lord, I will not cease declaring my faith.*

LESSON 19

Giving Thanks

A close friend of mine shared with me a sobering event at a previous pastorate. Under his ministry, the church grew from 400 to nearly 900 in attendance. They built a strong pastoral staff, wiped out all local debt, and established strategic relationships with people in the community. The church was healthy, strong, and growing in every manner. He was blessed by the church with a sabbatical in which he and his family enjoyed some much-needed rest.

Upon his return, the church board called for a special meeting, and they explained how God had spoken to them during his sabbatical. They said the Lord revealed that my friend was to resign from the church because pastoring at this church was holding him back. They believed he would flourish in a different pastorate. No doubt this came as a total shock to him, and he was faced with several options, including calling for a congregational vote or seeking direction from the district superintendent. He chose, instead, to honor the board. If they were hearing from the Lord, then he didn't want to hinder God. Four weeks later, he resigned after serving nearly a decade.

He never became offended or spoke negatively about the board; instead, he spoke positively about the church when friends and family questioned his resignation. Six months passed before another church extended an invitation to him to be their pastor. He purposed during that period to make a list of things he was grateful for, and after six months he compiled a gratitude list of 695 things. He explained to me that gratitude changed his attitude.

The Bible says, "Rejoice always; pray without ceasing; in everything give thanks; for this is God's will for you in Christ Jesus" (1 Thessalonians 5:16–18). These verses can be reduced to three present tense verbs implying continuous or reoccurring activities: rejoicing, praying, and thanking. Scholars also emphasize that "always," "without ceasing," and "in everything" strengthen the message that these actions should consistently characterize the Christian life. Furthermore, these activities fulfill the will of God for those in Christ.

What is God's will for you? To rejoice always, never stop praying, and keep giving thanks in whatever situation you may find yourself. My dear friend demonstrated that mandate as difficult as it was. He was thankful amid the situation, not necessarily for the circumstance. In verse 18, the little preposition (in) could be translated during. He remained thankful during a stressful and heartbreaking experience, and he made sure his words reflected his heart.

Jesus said, "Blessed are you when men hate you, and ostracize you, and insult you, and scorn your name as evil, for the sake of the Son of Man" (Luke 6:22). I've often heard people pray to be blessed or for those they care about to be blessed. But according to Jesus, the potential for blessing is being in a position where we are hated, ostracized, insulted, and scorned for His sake. In fact, Jesus continued, "Be glad in that day and leap *for joy*, for behold, your reward is great in heaven" (Luke 6:23a).

To be glad is a response of the will, not one of emotion, meaning it occurs by choice. Being glad (*chairo*) is rooted in what a person believes, not what they feel. When unfortunate situations or events occur, such as being asked to resign from a successful ministry, it doesn't change the truth of the gospel. If a person believes they still have favor with God regardless of what happens to them, then they have every reason to lift their praises to Him.

We have a powerful choice as to how we will respond when life treats us poorly or when troubling circumstances arise. I remember as a child hearing my parents sing in church about counting your blessings. Throughout my lifetime, that has been tested a time or two, and when I chose to give thanks instead of voicing my laments, the favor of God seemed to rest on me.

Paul and Silas were unjustly treated, beaten with rods, and imprisoned for liberating a demonically oppressed girl. At midnight, as they sat in darkness and in the stench of their dirty cell, the Bible says they were "singing hymns of praise to God" (Acts 16:25a). They weren't complaining or discussing their unfair treatment nor lamenting their circumstances. Instead, they chose to use their mouths to sing praises. Imagine what the other prisoners were thinking as Paul and Silas sat chained yet singing praises. The result of their praise was God shaking the prison with an earthquake and setting them and other prisoners free.

Imagine the impact this demonstration of praise had to have on these prisoners. How could someone ever forget that moment? The reality is that people are watching and listening. Your words spoken during unfair treatment, painful experiences, or disappointing news make a statement about your faith. They testify that God is greater than what is oppressing you, and your words might be the keys that liberate captives around you.

In the 1700s, John Wesley found himself in the middle of a raging storm while aboard a ship. While skilled sailors cried out in fear, Wesley observed a supernatural peace that rested upon a group of German Moravians. Instead of fear, they offered praises to God. This experience hounded Wesley and eventually led him to the infamous Aldersgate encounter where his heart was "strangely warmed." That experience led him to become one of England's greatest reformers, which resulted in worldwide spiritual ripples.

Much of Christendom owes a debt a gratitude to Wesley who is considered the father of the Wesleyan-Holiness Movement. But his ministry and its impact can be traced back to a group of believers giving thanks to God in the midst of dire circumstances.

Living with gratitude and thanksgiving in all situations will do three things. First, it will keep your attitude from becoming sour and negative. Giving praise to God may not change the immediate circumstances, but it will change you. Second, it will enable you to see possibilities over problems. Giving thanks in all situations changes your perspective so you start to see from God's viewpoint. You soon realize that "nothing will be impossible with God" (Luke 1:37). Third, it attracts people to you and the Christ in you.

When a believer refuses to give voice to all the ills of life, they become a welcome attraction to so many. May you learn to give thanks in all situations.

QUESTIONS

1. Would those closest to you say you are a grateful person? Why or why not?

2. What has your attitude been like over that last month? Describe.

3. What are some practical ways you can learn to give thanks in every situation?

If you choose to extend this lesson for one week, then complete the following questions and applications each day.

DAY 2 QUESTIONS
& Applications

1. Read 1 Thessalonians 5:14–18. What are your observations?

2. Describe how rejoicing and praying have to do with giving thanks.

3. What does it look like for you to give thanks in all things?

4. Prayer for today: *Lord, I'm living thankful in all situations.*

DAY 3 QUESTIONS
& Applications

1. Read Luke 6:20–23. What are your observations?

2. In verse 23, Jesus says to be glad. How can a person be glad when they experience what is described in verse 22?

3. Describe practical ways you can choose to be glad? What does that look like?

4. Prayer for today: *Lord, I choose to be glad in difficult seasons.*

DAY 4 — QUESTIONS & Applications

1. Read James 1:2–4. What are your observations?

2. In the NASB, verse 2 says, "Consider it all joy." What does that mean?

3. How are joy and giving thanks related?

4. Prayer for today: *Lord, I am choosing joy in the midst of my trials.*

DAY 5 — QUESTIONS & Applications

1. Read Acts 16:14–30. What are your observations?

2. According to verse 25, what were the other prisoners doing? How did giving praise to God affect the prisoners?

3. Prayer for today: *Lord, I will give praise to you all day long.*

DAY 6 QUESTIONS
& Applications

1. Reflecting on Acts 16:14–30, note what the jailer asked in verse 30. Describe how giving thanks and praise to God can lead people to Christ.

2. Are people attracted to Christ by your thanksgiving? If so, describe.

3. Prayer for today: *Lord, bring others to you through my thanksgiving.*

DAY 7 QUESTIONS
& Applications

1. What has the Holy Spirit taught you this week about thanksgiving?

2. What are some practical steps you can take to become a more thankful person?

3. Prayer for today: *Lord, teach me to be a thankful person.*

LESSON 20

A New Tongue

Throughout the New Testament, you will discover various things that have been made new through the redemptive work of Jesus Christ. The Greek word that is frequently used for this purpose is *kainos*. This term refers to something that has been made new in substance. A person can purchase something brand new, or something can be transformed into something new. Transformation is the idea behind the word *kainos*.

As I have read the Scripture, I have discovered twelve things that have been made new through the power of Christ. For example, 2 Corinthians 5:17 says we are a new creature. This refers to a person who, because of Christ, has begun a new life. The old things about a person are stripped off and through the power of redemption, they've become a new person. We still can recognize this person by their physical appearances, but spiritually they've been transformed into a new person.

Another example is found in John 13:34 where Jesus gave the disciples a new commandment to love as He loved. Jesus established a different standard of love; He inaugurated a new style of love, even for enemies, that His disciples had not yet experienced. Their understanding of love was warped by the traditions of the Pharisees. Consequently, they had "heard it said" to love their neighbors but hate their enemies (see Matthew 5:43). Through Christ, however, a new commandment was initiated that expanded the capacity of love to reflect the heart of God.

Christ changes everything, and He makes all things new including our tongue. In Mark 16:17–18, Jesus identified four signs (*semeion*) that would accompany a believer. During the time of the New Testament, official letters would be dispatched from a king to regions and subjects. The letters contained a seal that indicated they were authentic and royal letters, and it was called a *semeion*. Jesus used this word in conjunction with a believer and said they would be authentically identified by four signs, and one such sign is a new tongue.

The Greek word tongue (*glossa*) is translated language. New tongues (language) in Mark 16:17 are not to be confused with the tongues spoken at Pentecost in Acts 2:4, or the angelic tongues mentioned in 1 Corinthians 13:1, or even the tongues referred to in 1 Corinthians 14:14–15 that are often called private worship or prayer tongues. The new tongues Jesus said would accompany those who have believed refers to speech that is transformed, anointed, and empowered by the Lord.

The language of a believer is different because of his or her relationship with Christ. Our tongue becomes sourced with His Spirit; therefore, we speak with divine boldness. I had the privilege to hear the great revivalist Leonard Ravenhill challenge young Christians to speak with unction, a word that means power, urgency, and divine passion. If we are filled with the power of Christ, then our language will be different; it will be new and sourced with power.

Peter, empowered by the Holy Spirit, spoke with divine utterance in Acts 2:14 to a large crowd. The Bible says he "raised his voice and declared to them." Declare is a word that means to speak with boldness—unction. Compared to the way Peter spoke in the gospels, he now spoke with new tongues, and the result led to multitudes having their hearts pierced and being baptized (see Acts 2:37–41). Peter's words were so inspired by the Spirit of God that people cried out, "Brethren, what shall we do?"

In Acts 4:13, Peter and John spoke with boldness to the religious leaders. Although they were uneducated and untrained, the religious leaders realized these two disciples had been with Jesus. The evidence that gave them away was their unction. In other words, they spoke with new tongues. In Acts 4:31, after the disciples prayed, they were all filled with the Holy Spirit, and this resulted in speaking the Word of God with boldness. The Bible says, "With great boldness the apostles were giving testimony to the resurrection of the Lord Jesus" (Acts 4:33a). I believe these are examples of speaking with new tongues.

I'm reminded of an event where I was preaching to a large group of teenagers. Many of these teens came from secular schools and broken homes, and a few had little to no church background. I realized these kids needed to have a radical encounter with the presence of God if they were to leave this conference spiritually changed. I, and others with me, prayed along with Paul who said, "And *pray* on my behalf, that utterance may be given to me in the opening of my mouth, to make known with boldness the mystery of the gospel" (Ephesians 6:19).

Paul wanted to preach with boldness, which means to speak freely and unhindered with unction. I propose that he desired to declare the gospel with new tongues. If Christ didn't source his mouth, then transformation would not have occurred in his audience. The Holy Spirit inspired my preaching and I spoke with boldness during that youth conference, and a hundred plus teenagers experienced transformational encounters with the presence of God.

I desire to speak with a new tongue. I want my language to bear witness to the fact that I'm an intimate disciple of Jesus Christ. Before I was a Christ follower, I spoke with old tongues. My language was filthy, coarse, and worldly (see Ephesians 5:4). My words reflected the nature of my heart. But Jesus not only gave me a new heart, but also He gave me a new tongue. Does your speech give evidence that you are an intimate follower of Christ?

Besides giving your life to Christ, ask the Lord to sanctify your tongue. I was preaching at a conference, and during the invitation to come forward for ministry, a gentleman approached me and asked if I could agree in prayer that he receive a new tongue. He desired to have a sanctified tongue so he would speak with inspiration and life. So, we prayed together for that to occur. I believe it's a great request.

Spending much time in the presence of Jesus is critical to speaking with a new tongue. You will always be like the person you spend the most time with. Spend time with Him by reading and soaking in the Scriptures. Listen to the Word when you drive to work or walk on a treadmill. I stated this before, but your mouth will speak what your heart is full of. Remain full of His Word, and your language will remain new, bold, fresh, and alive.

May Jesus give you bold, inspired, new tongues.

QUESTIONS

1. Describe what you believe it means to speak with a new tongue (bold speech). Can you identify a few people you know who speak in that manner?

2. What can you do to speak with a new tongue? Describe your process.

3. Have you ever experienced speaking to someone, and the presence of God touched them or filled the room in an extraordinary way? If so, describe your experience.

> If you choose to extend this lesson for one week, then complete
> the following questions and applications each day.

DAY 2 — QUESTIONS & Applications

1. Read Acts 4:1–13. What are your observations?

2. Reflecting on this passage, how was boldness demonstrated?

3. Prayer for today: *Lord, I will be bold to speak your word.*

DAY 3 — QUESTIONS & Applications

1. Read Acts 4:13–31. What are your observations? What threatened their boldness?

2. Reflecting on this passage, how was boldness demonstrated?

3. Prayer for today: *Lord, I will not be intimated by anything.*

DAY 4 — QUESTIONS & Applications

1. What is the difference between boldness and abrasiveness?

2. What is the difference between "old" tongues and "new" tongues? Do your words reflect an old or new tongue? Explain.

3. Prayer for today: *Lord, I will reflect Christ in my words.*

DAY 5 — QUESTIONS & Applications

1. Read Ephesians 5:3–8. What are your observations?

2. How do the words you speak give evidence (a sign) that you are a believer?

3. What do you think it means to speak with an anointing?

4. Prayer for today: *Lord, let your Holy Spirit use my mouth.*

DAY 6 — QUESTIONS & Applications

1. Read Ephesians 5:18–20. What are your observations?

2. Reflecting on this passage, how are new tongues being expressed? What is the relationship between being drunk with wine and filled with the Spirit?

3. Prayer for today: *Lord, I want to speak under the influence of the Spirit.*

DAY 7 — QUESTIONS & Applications

1. Reflecting on this week, what have you learned about new tongues?

2. What practical steps will you take to speak with boldness and unction?

3. Read Ephesians 6:19. Make this your prayer.

4. Prayer for today: *Lord, will have unction when I speak the gospel.*

LESSON 21

Grumble Fast

In March of 2017, I stood before the church I was pastoring and announced that I was going on a special fast. I realize we shouldn't publicize our deeds of righteousness, but this was a different kind of fast and I was sure I needed the accountability of my church. I'm no longer pastoring that church, but my fast continues to this day. Before I explain what the fast is, let me take you to the Scripture I was studying that prompted my announcement.

In 1 Corinthians 10, Paul explained to the church in Corinth that he didn't want them to be ignorant about the evil deeds of the Israelites in the Old Testament. There were lessons to be learned from their lives that the Corinthians needed to be aware of, and they are examples for us in this very hour too. Paul identified four major sins that led to the Israelite's demise. Those four sins are: idolatry, immorality, testing the Lord, and grumbling.

Grumbling? Are you serious? Grumbling is a way of life for most of us. It's what we do to make small talk with our barber or beautician. We grumble about the weather, economy, politics, church leadership, and even the traffic. But the Bible indicates grumbling is a serious sin that aligns us to the work of darkness.

Here's how the verse reads, "Nor grumble, as some of them did, and were destroyed by the destroyer" (1 Corinthians 10:10). God's people were destroyed for grumbling, and this is one of the major sins that was written down for our instruction (see 1 Corinthians 10:11). In other words, grumbling is a serious sin in the eyes of God, the Israelites participated in it, but He desires for us to abstain from it.

Who could argue with the other three sins? Those sins are obvious problems from my perspective, but I would have never considered grumbling as something that could be detrimental to my spiritual life. The word grumble (*gongyzo*) means to groan or murmur despair, or to speak complaints under your breath against someone or something. One expositor stated that grumbling comes from our agreement with something that is contrary to God's will. It's a symptom of faithlessness, and so our mouth declares our agreement with something displeasing to the Lord.

Miriam and Aaron complained and grumbled against Moses (Numbers 12:1–10). The Bible says that Miriam was a prophetess (Exodus 15:20). Therefore, she was prophesying against an appointed leader, and God heard her complaints. God's anger burned against Miriam and Aaron, the priest and prophet, and Miriam's skin turned leprous. We might question what happens to the body of Christ when churches are filled with grumbling, complaining members. Perhaps the health of our churches is impaired because we grumble against the leadership, finances, facility, music, or its people.

Because of grumbling, the Israelites "were destroyed by the destroyer" (1 Corinthians 10:10). The word destroyer (*olothreutes*) refers to a venomous snake. A similar word appears in Exodus 12:23 referring to the death angel sent to smite those not covered by the blood. The Israelite's grumbling was so serious to God that it severed their covenant with Him. Therefore, they were spiritually uncovered and became vulnerable to the enemy. Their words aligned them with death. In the same manner, our words indicate with whom or what we are aligning ourselves.

In Matthew 12:24, Jesus was accused of being sourced by Beelzebul, the ruler of demons. Beelzebul is the god of flies and gnats. Generally, flies and gnats are attracted to dead things, such as an animal along the side of the road. I started thinking about lifeless words that we speak. If we speak life or death (see Proverbs 18:21), then what happens when the prince of demons—the god of flies and gnats—hears dead words? Maybe the enemy fills the atmosphere to feast on barren, lifeless words uttered from our mouths in a spew of complaints.

Imagine believers standing in a lobby of a church only moments before a service begins, and they are grumbling about their employer or an event in the news. Perhaps worship is hindered because the destroyer is having a banquet of lifeless words in the church. Think with me about the atmosphere of your home, your office at work, or a conference room where your leadership team meets. Are your words creating an atmosphere that is attractive to the enemy?

The Holy Spirit began probing my heart about this subject matter. I realized that the words I released from my mouth affected the atmosphere, and I no longer wanted to attract the prince of darkness into my life. Frankly, I grumbled about everything, and it had to stop. As we have already discussed, Jesus only spoke words of life (John 6:63), and if I'm an intimate follower of Him, then grumbling could no longer be part of my speech.

So, I stood before my church in 2017, confessing the sin of grumbling and announcing that Sunday was the beginning a grumble fast. My intentions were to eliminate all grumbling from my life for several months. To be honest, it was hard. I've fasted meals, sweets, coffee, and certain foods, but I never fasted from grumbling and complaining. Did I fail a time or two? Sure did. And members from our church held me accountable. After several months it caught on, and many joined me in the grumble fast.

To this day, I'm still fasting from grumbling. I've written about this subject and taught about it in several churches across the nation. I've invited hundreds of people to join me, and some have committed to this as a lifelong process. My grumble fast is what prompted the writing of this book, and at the end of this lesson, I will invite you to join me.

No one needs to grumble. We do it by choice. It's been said that if we sow an act, we will reap a habit. And if we sow a habit, we will reap a character. Grumbling has become the character of many people simply because they started sowing the act years ago. What if you stopped? What if you started sowing gratitude instead of complaints or thanksgiving instead of grumbling? I will tell you from experience that it will change your life.

Are you ready to join with me in a life without grumbling?

QUESTIONS

1. Do you know someone, other than Jesus, who doesn't grumble? If so, describe his or her life.

2. When it comes to complaining and grumbling, how would those closest to you describe your life?

3. Will you fast from grumbling? What are some practical ways that can help you remain faithful to your grumble fast?

> If you choose to extend this lesson for one week, then complete the following questions and applications each day.

DAY 2

QUESTIONS
& Applications

1. Read 1 Corinthians 10:1–13. What is the Holy Spirit saying to you?

2. Why was Israel destroyed for grumbling? Are there consequences for our grumbling? If so, describe.

3. Prayer for today: *Lord, thank you for my grumble fast.*

DAY 3   QUESTIONS & Applications

1. Read Philippians 2:14–15. What are your observations?

2. How can a person do all things without grumbling?

3. If you have chosen to fast from grumbling, how are you doing? What things help your fast? What situations or people hinder your fast?

4. Prayer for today: *Lord, my mouth will not speak complaints.*

DAY 4   QUESTIONS & Applications

1. What is the atmosphere of your home like? What about at work? What about at church?

2. What can you do to improve the atmosphere where you work or live?

3. Is the enemy attracted to things you say? Why or why not?

4. Prayer for today: *Lord, may my words attract your presence.*

DAY 5 — QUESTIONS & Applications

1. Read Numbers 12:1–15. What are your observations?

2. Note verse 9, why was God so angry?

3. Are there spiritual consequences in our lives when we grumble? If so, explain.

4. Prayer for today: *Lord, I will not speak against other people.*

DAY 6 — QUESTIONS & Applications

1. Why do you believe people grumble so easily?

2. Do you believe difficult people and challenging circumstances make us grumble? Why or why not?

3. What is the opposite of grumbling?

4. Prayer for today: *Lord, I will become known as a grateful person in all situations.*

DAY 7

QUESTIONS
& Applications

1. What has the Holy Spirit taught you this week about grumbling? Have you avoided grumbling this week? Why or why not?

2. How can you describe unpleasant situations without grumbling? Are you able to watch the news or read about world events and not grumble? Explain.

3. Will you remain on a lifetime grumble fast? Why or why not?

4. Prayer for today: *Lord, empower me from this day forward to never grumble.*

EPILOGUE

Proverbs 18:21 (NLT) says, "The tongue can bring death or life; those who love to talk will reap the consequences." Whether you are chatty or quiet, you will always reap the consequences of the words you speak. As we have said from the beginning, your words are not neutral.

Together we have examined throughout this book the potentially damaging consequences your words can have on you and others. Hopefully by now, with the help of the Holy Spirit, you have begun adjusting your life so that you will not speak with a tongue of death but a tongue of life.

I want to close by emphasizing the positive consequences of speaking life. All of creation came into existence because God spoke a word. The psalmist wrote, "By the word of the Lord the heavens were made" (Psalm 33:6a). The nature of God's words is life-giving. We have the privilege to speak in the same manner. Our words can heal, restore, and instill life. We can speak words that mend the brokenhearted, impart hope to the fearful, and bring strength to weary souls.

Most of all, we can use words to announce the good news of Jesus Christ. I'll never forget the first time I shared the gospel with another person. Tears ran down his face as he experienced God's unconditional love. The Lord cleansed his sin and filled him with His Spirit, and then we celebrated together with shouts of joy. From that moment on, I realized the powerful potential of the gospel.

The greatest need in this hour is for people to hear the message of Jesus Christ. Jesus began His ministry urging people to repent and believe the gospel. We have the privilege and assignment to urge people to do the same thing. I want my words to be used to direct and lead people to Christ. I want to clearly proclaim that there is no other name under heaven by which we can be saved but through Christ alone (see Acts 4:12). I want the consequences of my words to be multitudes of people coming into an eternal relationship with Jesus Christ as their Lord and Savior.

Ponder, the next time you are about to speak, the potential eternal benefit or consequences released through your words. Your mouth carries life and death, how will you use it?

ABOUT

Becoming Love
Ministries Association

Since 2008, Dan Bohi has been answering the call to awaken the church of Jesus Christ to the power, purity, and freedom of the Spirit-filled life, found, realized, experienced, and exhibited in the lives of believers in the book of Acts. He has traversed the country from coast to coast crossing denominational lines and teaching the timeless truths from God's Word. Pastors and church leaders have confirmed that thousands have experienced encounters with the presence of God in his meetings, and congregations have been transformed.

To help fulfill the call to awaken churches, Dan founded an international ministry called, *Becoming Love Ministries Association* (BLMA). This ministry is comprised of a team of full-time ministers, teachers, and evangelists who help impart kingdom truths through writing, teaching, training, equipping, and traveling across the nations holding crusades and conferences in denominations and churches of all sizes. To date, BLMA has been used by God to touch tens of thousands of people with the gospel across the United States and in other nations.

Rob McCorkle and his wife, Cindy, travel full-time for BLMA speaking in conferences and churches, imparting kingdom truths to pastors, leaders, and congregations across denominational lines. He is the author of *Bridging the Great Divide* and *Elevate*, and he co-authored *Holiness and Healing* with Dan Bohi. For scheduling of team members, information, or resources, please contact:

Jim Williams (Executive Director)
7905 North West 48th Street
Bethany, OK 73008
JimWilliams@BecomingLoveMinistries.com
BecomingLoveMinistries.com
FireSchoolMinistries.com (Resources by Rob McCorkle)

NOTES

1. Henry Cloud and John Townsend, *Boundaries* (Grand Rapids, MI: Zondervan Publishing House, 1992), 214.

2. Frank Viola, "Two-Faced Christians," Beyond Evangelical, January 25, 2018, accessed on April 8, 2020, https://frankviola.org/2018/01/25/twofaced/.

3. There is enormous research on this topic. One such article is entitled, "The Power of Words and Your Health." See https://www.kirbyhealth.org/about/news/2016/december/the-power-of-words-and-your-health/. See also Carolyn Leaf, *Who Switched Off My Brain?* (Dallas, TX: Switch on Your Brain USA, Inc., 2008).

Made in the USA
Monee, IL
17 December 2022

21826061R00105